SAY IT IN
ARABIC
(EGYPTIAN DIALECT)

by Farouk El-Baz

D0444399

Dover Publications, Inc.
New York

Say It in Arabic (*Egyptian Dialect*) is a new work, first published by Dover Publications, Inc., in 1968.

Standard Book Number: 486-22026-5
Library of Congress Catalog Card Number: 67-17506

Manufactured in the United States of America

Dover Publications, Inc.
180 Varick Street
New York, N. Y. 10014

CONTENTS

CONTENTS

CONTENTS

INTRODUCTION

Arabic is the language of over eighty million people who inhabit a vast area extending throughout North Africa and the Middle East. The language originated in the Arabian Peninsula and spread north and west with the rise of Islam.

Spoken Arabic has deviated from the original language in most parts of the Arab World. The situation is that of a classical language and various dialects. However, the grammatical rules of spoken Arabic are based largely on those of the classical language. Variations in dialects involve mainly modifications in the pronunciation of a few letters, as well as local preferences for certain terms and expressions, mostly Arabized terms derived from English and the Romance languages.

Spoken Arabic today can be classified into six major divisions:

1. THE CLASSICAL LANGUAGE: Since it originated in the Arabian Peninsula, and has undergone only negligible changes, this language is still the medium of daily expression of all the inhabitants of that region, both nomads and town dwellers. Classical Arabic is also the language of the nomadic communities throughout the Arab World. This means that "corruption" of the language flourished in cities and towns, and therefore dialects are one trait of urbanism in the Arab World.

1

2. The Mediterranean Dialect: This dialect is spoken in the geographical region which lies to the north of the Arabian Peninsula and includes the modern states of Jordan, Israel, Lebanon and Syria. Apart from some local variations within this region, the basic pattern of the dialect remains the same. Among the varieties of spoken Arabic, it is about the closest to the classical language.

3. The Iraqi Dialect: This is a variant of the dialect just mentioned. Its distinguishing feature is the frequent incorporation of Kurdish, Persian and Turkish sounds and expressions.

4. The Northern Nile Valley Dialect: The widely known "Cairo dialect" is used today in most parts of Lower Egypt. It may be the dialect that has deviated most from the classical language. A unique characteristic of this dialect is the replacement of the *th* (theh), *j* (jeem), *z* (thal) and *q* (qahf) sounds by *s*, hard *g, d* and ', respectively.*

5. The Southern Nile Valley Dialect: The Arabic spoken in southern Egypt and in the Sudan is similar to the "Cairo dialect" but closer to the classical language. It is unique in the use of a hard *g* for the *q* consonant. It is the dialect which is least "contaminated" with foreign terms and expressions.

6. The North African Dialect: The North

---

* The *q* sound is still heard in such words as *qah-MOOS* (dictionary) and *moo-SEE-qah* (music), as well as in the name of Islam's holy book, the Qur'an.

African Arabs, living in Libya, Tunisia, Algeria and Morocco, also have a dialect of their own. Although still based on the classical language, it is distinguished by the incorporation of terms and expressions from the Romance languages, as well as some from the Berber tongues.

This booklet is intended to be of use to Americans visiting or temporarily residing in the Arab World. Therefore, it was important to employ an easy-to-learn but also widely understood dialect. The "Cairo dialect" was chosen for these two reasons. It is the simplest of all the spoken dialects, especially as far as phonetics is concerned. While linguistically "incorrect," its simplicity springs from the tendency to use one sound for more than one letter of the classical alphabet. This fact makes the dialect the easiest for English-speaking people to learn, since the outcome of this tendency is the replacement of some difficult sounds. In addition to this, Cairenes have, more than other Arab speakers, incorporated into their dialect several terms that stem from English and the Romance languages rather than from the classical Arabic. Moreover, Cairo has been and remains one of the most vital cultural centers of the entire area. Its dialect is therefore the most widely understood in the rest of the Arab World.

Notes on the Use of This Book

1. The material in this book has been selected chiefly to teach you many essential phrases,

sentences and questions for travel. It will serve as a direct and interesting introduction to the spoken language if you are beginning your study. The sentences will be useful to you whether or not you go on to further study. With the aid of a dictionary, many pattern sentences included here will answer innumerable needs, for example: "Is there a [pharmacy] here?" The brackets indicate that substitutions can be made for these words with the use of a bilingual dictionary. In other sentences, for the words in square brackets you can substitute the words immediately following (in the same sentence or in the indented entries below it). For example, the entry

What is the charge [per hour] per day?

provides two sentences: "What is the charge per hour?" and "What is the charge per day?" Three sentences are provided by the entry

I shall take a room [for one night].
——— for a week or so.
——— for two persons.

As your Arabic vocabulary grows, you will find that you can express an increasingly wide range of thoughts by the proper substitution of words in these model sentences.

2. In Arabic there are many more gender changes than there are in English. This is particularly true of verb and adjective forms, although

gender affects pronouns and other parts of speech as well. The rules of gender are complex, and *Say It in Arabic* does not attempt to explain these rules and their use. To avoid ambiguity and error, all appropriate sentences are followed by these abbreviations to indicate clearly the correct gender:

(M.)	male speaking to anyone
(F.)	female speaking to anyone
(TO M.)	anyone speaking to a male
(TO F.)	anyone speaking to a female
(M. TO M.)	male speaking to male
(F. TO F.)	female speaking to female

Wherever advisable, we have given full sentences in two forms (male and female speaking, or else male and female addressed). Where no gender is indicated the statement may be considered general; that is, it may be spoken by male or female to male or female.

Other abbreviations used are:

(TO GR.)	anyone speaking to a group
(MASC.)	masculine*
(FEM.)	feminine*
(LIT.)	literally
(SING.)	singular
(PL.)	plural

3. You will find the extensive index at the end of the book especially helpful. Capitalized items

---

* These abbreviations are used, for instance, to show whether a "friend" or a "manager" is a man or a woman.

in the index refer to section headings and give the number of the page on which the section begins. All other numbers refer to *entry numbers*. All the entries in the book are numbered consecutively.

PRONUNCIATION

The phonetic transcription used in this book should be pronounced as if it were English. Special attention should be given to five sounds which have no English equivalents. These are listed below under the heading "Consonants," and should be studied carefully and thoroughly. When using the transcription, read the words and phrases smoothly, without syllable breaks. Syllables to be emphasized are printed in capital letters.

VOWELS

Vowels are given below in a separate list for purposes of quick reference. In forming the Arabic long vowels, continue the pure sound of the short vowel, without producing a diphthong (*ay-ee* or *oh-oo*) as in English.

TRANSCRIPTION	EXAMPLES
a	Short; like the *a* in "cat" or "hat."
ah	Long; like the *a* in "far" or "father."
ay	Long; like the *a* in "make" or the *ay* in "play."

TRANSCRIPTION	EXAMPLES
e	Short; like the *e* in "h*e*n" or "p*e*n."
ee	Long; like the *e* in "m*e*" or "th*e*me."
i	Short; like the *i* in "*i*ll" or "f*i*t."
ī	Long; like the *i* in "*i*ce" or "sm*i*le."
u	Short; like the *u* in "l*u*ck" or "d*u*ck."
ū	Long; like the *u* in "f*u*ll" or "p*u*ll."
o	Short; like the *o* in "*o*dd" or "p*o*d."
oh	Short; like the *o* in "h*o*le" or "h*o*me."
oo	Long; like the *oo* in "n*oo*n" or "f*oo*d."
ow	Long; like the *ow* in "c*ow*" or "h*ow*."

Consonants

For a complete list of the Arabic consonants, the reader is referred to the alphabet (p. 153). In the following list we give only those consonants used in the transcription the sounds of which cannot be fully conveyed by English letters. Therefore, all letters not listed are to be pronounced in accordance with the usual American usage.

TRANSCRIPTION	EXPLANATION
'	This represents the glottal stop, the gulp-like sound, formed in the back of the throat, heard (for instance) in place of the omitted *tt* in the Cockney pronunciation of "better" or the colloquial New York pronunciation of "bottle." Say "a-a-a-a-a-a" moderately rapidly and observe the muscular "click" accompanying the beginning of each *a*-sound—that is the glottal stop, shown in this book by the apostrophe (').
g	Always hard, like the *g* in "*go*" or "*get*."
h̄	A strongly aspirated *h*; a hard guttural sound produced in the back of the mouth. It can be enunciated by whispering the *h* as loudly as possible.
kh	A hard guttural sound similar to that produced when one clears the throat. The familiar sound closest to it is the *ch* in the German word "*Achtung*" and the Scottish word "lo*ch*."
q	Used in only a few words. A *k*-sound formed very far back in the throat.

TRANSCRIPTION	EXPLANATION
r	Unlike the English r, it is trilled with the tip of the tongue like the Italian or Spanish r. It can best be produced by taking a breath and blowing it out with the tongue against the palate.
$\bar{r}$	A guttural consonant pronounced in the back of the throat, equivalent to the French (Parisian) r. It is very similar to the sound produced by gargling.

PERSONAL PRONOUNS

1. I.
A-nah.

2. He.
HOO-wah.

3. She.
HEE-yah.

4. It.
HOO-wah (referring to masculine noun).
HEE-yah (referring to feminine noun).

5. We.
EH̄-nah.

6. They.
HOHM-mah.

7. You.
EN-tah. (TO M.)
EN-tee. (TO F.)
EN-too. (TO GR.)

GENERAL EXPRESSIONS

8. Yes.
Ī-wah.

9. No.
la'.

10. Perhaps.
YIM-kin.

11. Please.
min-FAHD-luk. (TO M.)
min-FAHD-lik. (TO F.)
min-fahd-LOH-kŭm. (TO GR.)

12. Excuse me.
es-MAH̄-lee. (TO M.)
es-mah-H̄EE-lee. (TO F.)
es-mah-H̄OO-lee. (TO GR.)

13. I am sorry.
A-nah A-sif. (M.)
A-nah AS-fah. (F.)

14. We are sorry.
EH̄-nah as-FEEN.

15. Thanks a lot.
alf SHŬK-re.

16. Don't mention it (You're welcome).
el-AH-foo.

17. Never mind.
mah-LESH.*

18. There isn't.
ma-FEESH.

19. Is that so!
ya-sa-LAM!

---

* This is a much used expression and is also equivalent to:
that's too bad; it doesn't matter; forget it; etc.

20. Good.
KWĬ-yis.

21. Bad.
mish KWĬ-yis.

22. What?
ay?

23. When?
EM-tah?

24. Where?
fayn?

25. Here.
HE-nah.

26. There.
he-NAK.

27. Who?
meen?

28. Why?
lay?

29. Why not?
lay la'?

30. How?
iz ZĬ?

31. How many?
Kam?

32. How much?
bee-KAM?

33. How long?
ad-dee-AY?

34. Okay!
TĬ-yib!

35. Who is it?
meen?

36. Just a minute.
dee-EE-a WAĤ-da.

37. Come in (formal).
et-FAHD-dull. (TO M.)
et-fahd-DUL-lee. (TO F.)
et-fahd-DUL-loo. (TO GR.)

38. Come in (informal).
od-KHŬLL. (TO M.)
od-KHŬL-lee. (TO F.)
od-KHŬL-loo. (TO GR.)

39. What is the matter?
ay el-ĥe-KA-ya?

40. What do you want?
AH-wiz ay? (TO M.)
OW-zah ay? (TO F.)
ow-ZEEN ay? (TO GR.)

41. Look out!
ĤA-sib! (TO M.)
ĤAS-bee! (TO F.)
ĤAS-boo! (TO GR.)

42. Listen!
ES-mah! (TO M.)
es-MAH-ee! (TO F.)
es-MAH-oo! (TO GR.)

43. Take care!
KHAL-lee BA-lak! (TO M.)
KHAL-lee BA-lik! (TO F.)
KHAL-lee BAL-koo! (TO GR.)

44. Hello! (Hi!)
as-sa-LA-moo ah-LAY-kūm.*

45. Hello! (in reply to the foregoing)
wi-ah-LAY-kūm is-sa-LAM.*

46. Good morning.
sah-BAH̄ el-KHAY-re.†

47. Good night.
tes-BAH̄ AH-lah KHAY re. (TO M.)
tes-BAH̄-ĥee AH-lah KHAY-re. (TO F.)
tes-BAH̄-ĥoo AH-lah KHAY-re. (TO GR.)

48. Good night. (in reply to the foregoing)
WEN-tah min-AHL el-KHAY-re. (TO M.)
WEN-tee min-AHL el-KHAY-rc. (TO F.)
WEN-too min-AHL el-KHAY-re. (TO GR.)

---

* The literal translation of the expression is: " May peace
be with you!" and of the reply to it: "And may peace be
with you!" When said to one person it connotes peace of
mind; when said to a group it implies peace of action.

† One can reply to this greeting by repeating the expression. However, a much-used reply is *sah-BAH in-NOOR*,
which implies: " May your day be bright."

YOURSELF

49. I am an American.
A-nah am-ree-KA-nee. (M.)
A-nah am-ree-ka-NEE-ya. (F.)

50. We are Americans.
EH̄-nah am-ree-KAN.

51. My name is ———.
A-nah IS-mee ———.

52. I am [thirty] years old.
A-nah SIN-nee [ta-la-TEEN] SA-na.

53. I am staying at the Nile Hilton.
A-nah NA-zill fill "Hilton."

54. I am a student.
A-nah TAH-lib. (M.)
A-nah tah-LI-ba. (F.)

55. We are students.
EH̄-nah TAH-lah-bah. (M.)
EH̄-nah tah-li-BAT. (F.)

56. I am a teacher.
A-nah moo-DAR-riss. (M.)
A-nah moo-dar-RIS-sa. (F.)

57. We are teachers.
EH̄-nah moo-dar-ris-SEEN. (M.)
EH̄-nah moo-dar-ris-SAT. (F.)

58. I am a businessman.
A-nah TA-ger.

59. I am here to study.
A-nah HE-nah lid-de-RAH-sa.

60. I am making a tour of the Arab World.
A-nah fee REH-la li-zee-YAH-ret ed-DOO-wahl el-ah-rah-BEE-ya.

61. I am here on a scientific trip.
A-nah HE-nah fee REH-la el-MEE-ya.

62. I am here on a business trip.
A-nah HE-nah lit-tee-GAH-rah.

63. I am leaving for Aswan tomorrow [morning] [afternoon].
A-nah RAH-yeh ahs-WAHN BOK-rah [is-SOB-hc] [bahd id-DOH-re].

64. I am cold [warm].
A-nah bar-DAN [hahr-RAHN]. (M.)
A-nah bar-DA-na [hahr-RAH-nah]. (F.)

65. We are cold [warm].
EH-nah bar-da-NEEN [hahr-rah-NEEN].

66. I am hungry [thirsty].
A-nah gah-AHN [aht-SHAHN]. (M.)
A-nah gah-AH-nah [aht-SHAH-nah]. (F.)

67. We are hungry [thirsty].
EH-nah gah-ah-NEEN [at-shah-NEEN].

68. I am busy [tired].
A-nah mash-ROOL [ta-BAN]. (M.)
A-nah mash-ROO-la [ta-BA-na]. (F.)

69. We are busy [tired].
EH-nah mash-roo-LEEN [ta-ba-NEEN].

70. I am in a hurry.
A-nah mis-TA-gill. (M.)
A-nah mis-ta-GIL-la. (F.)

71. We are in a hurry.
EH̄-nah mis-ta-gil-LEEN.

72. I am glad [sad].
A-nah fahr-H̄AHN [zah-LAN]. (M.)
A-nah fahr-H̄AH-nah [zah-LA-na]. (F.)

73. We are glad [sad].
EH̄-nah fahr-h̄ah-NEEN [zah-la-NEEN].

74. I am sick [fine].
A-nah ī-YAN [KWĪ-yis]. (M.)
A-nah ī-YA-na [kwī-YI-sa]. (F.)

75. We are sick [fine].
EH̄-nah ī-ya-NEEN [kwī-yis-SEEN].

76. I am happy.
A-nah mahb-SOOT. (M.)
A-nah mahb-SOO-tah. (F.)

77. We are happy.
EH̄-nah mahb-soo-TEEN.

SOCIAL CONVERSATION

78. How do you do?
AH-lahn wah SAH-lahn.

79. I am glad to know (or meet) you.
ta-shahr-RUF-nah.

80. How are you?
   iz-ZĪ-yak? (TO M.)
   iz-ZĪ-yik? (TO F.)
   iz-zī-YOH-kūm? (TO GR.)

81. How are things?
   iz-ZĪ el-aḥ-WAHL?

82. Fine (All right).
   el-ḤAHM-doo lil-LA.*

83. How is [your family]?
   iz-ZĪ [el-AY-lah]?

84. ——— your wife?
   ——— el-ma-DAM?

85. How are [your parents]?
   iz-ZĪ [el-wah-lee-DAYN]?

86. ——— your children?
   ——— el-ow-LAD?

87. May I introduce [Mr. ———]?
   a-ad-DIM-lak [es-SĪ-yed ———]? (TO M.)
   a-ad-DIM-lik [es-SĪ-yed ———]? (TO F.)
   a-ad-dim-LOH-kūm [es-SĪ-yed ———]?
                                    (TO GR.)

88. ——— Mrs. ———?
   ——— es-sī-YI-da ———?

---

* The literal translation of the Arabic words would be:
"Thanks to God!" It is usually not necessary to answer the
inquiry by saying "Fine, thanks, and you?" for the in-
quirer would be just as satisfied that you are thanking God,
which connotes being fine.

89. ——— **Miss** ———?
——— el-a-NIS-sa ———?

90. ——— **my mother?**
——— wal-DI-tee (OR ŪM-mee)?

91. ——— **my father?**
——— WAL-dee (OR ah-BOO-ya)?

92. ——— **my wife?**
——— me-RAH-tee?

93. ——— **my husband?**
——— GOH-zee?

94. ——— **my son?**
——— IB-nee?

95. ——— **my daughter?**
——— BEN-tee?

96. ——— **my brother?**
——— ah-KHOO-ya?

97. ——— **my sister?**
——— ŪKH-tee?

98. ——— **my uncle (father's brother)?**
——— AHM-mee?

99. ——— **my aunt (father's sister)?**
——— ahm-MI-tee?

100. ——— **my uncle (mother's brother)?**
——— KHA-lee?

101. ——— **my aunt (mother's sister)?**
——— KHAL-tee?

102. ——— my cousin (father's brother's
     son)?
     ——— ibn AHM-mee?

103. ——— my cousin (father's brother's
     daughter)?
     ——— bent AHM-mee?

104. ——— my cousin (mother's brother's
     son)?
     ——— ibn KHA-lee?

105. ——— my cousin (mother's brother's
     daughter)?
     ——— bent KHA-lee?

106. ——— my cousin (father's sister's son)?
     ——— ibn ahm-MI-tee?

107. ——— my cousin (father's sister's
     daughter)?
     ——— bent ahm-MI-tee?

108. ——— my cousin (mother's sister's
     son)?
     ——— ibn KHAL-tee?

109. ——— my cousin (mother's sister's
     daughter)?
     ——— bent KHAL-tee?

110. ——— my nephew (brother's son)?
     ——— ibn al-KHOO-ya?

111. ——— my nephew (sister's son)?
     ——— ibn ŪKH-tee?

112. —— my niece (brother's daughter)?
—— bent ah-KHOO-ya?

113. —— my niece (sister's daughter)?
—— bent ŪKH-tee?

114. —— my father-in-law?
—— ḥa-MA-ya?

115. —— my mother-in-law?
—— ḥa-MA-tee?

116. —— my son-in-law?
—— gohz BEN-tee?

117. —— my daughter-in-law?
—— me-RAHT IB-nee?

118. —— my stepfather?
—— gohz ŪM-mee?

119. —— my stepmother?
—— me-RAHT ah-BOO-ya?

120. —— my relative?
—— a-REE-bee? (MASC.)
—— a-RIB-tee? (FEM.)

121. —— my friend?
—— SAḤ-bee? (MASC.)
—— saḥ-BI-tee? (FEM.)

122. **What is your name?**
EN-tah IS-mak ay? (TO M.)
EN-tee IS-mik ay? (TO F.)

123. What is your job?
EN-tah be-tish-TA-ṟal ay? (TO M.)
EN-tee be-tish-TA-ṟa-lee ay? (TO F.)

124. Where is your office?
el-MAK-tab be-TA-ahk fayn? (TO M.)
el-MAK-tab be-TA-ik fayn? (TO F.)

125. Where is your company?
ish-SHIR-ka be-TA-tak fayn? (TO M.)
ish-SHIR-ka be-TA-tik fayn? (TO F.)

126. What are you doing tonight?
ḥah-TAY-mill ay el-lay-LA-dee? (TO M.)
ḥah-tay-MI-lee ay el-lay-LA-dee? (TO F.)

127. Would you like to join us?
te-ḤEBB TEE-gee may-AH-nah? (TO M.)
te-ḤIB-bee TEE-gee may-AH-nah? (TO F.)

128. Please have a seat.
et-FAHD-dull oh'-OD. (TO M.)
et-fahd-DUL-lee oh'-OD-dee. (TO F.)

129. Who is [that boy] that man?
meen [el-WA-lad da] ir-RAH-gill da?

130. Who is [that girl] that lady?
meen [el-BENT dee] is-SIT dee?

131. Give me your [address] telephone number.
id-DEE-nee [en-WAH-nak] NEM-rit te-le-FOH-nak. (TO M.)
id-DEE-nee [en-WAH-nik] NEM-rit te-le-FOH-nik. (TO F.)

132. Give my regards to your [boy friend] girl friend.
sal-LIM-lee AH-lah [SAH̱-buk] saẖ-BI-tak. (TO M.)

sal-li-MEE-lee AH-lah [SAH̱-bik] saẖ-BI-tik. (TO F.)

133. I have enjoyed myself [very much].
A-nah it-bah-SUT [GID-dan].

134. We have enjoyed ourselves [very much].
EH̱-nah it-bah-SUT-nah [GID-dan].

135. I love you.
A-nah ba-H̱EB-bak. (TO M.)
A-nah ba-H̱EB-bik. (TO F.)

TO BE UNDERSTOOD

136. Do you speak English?
EN-tah be-tit-KAL-lim en-ge-LEE-zee? (TO M.)

EN-tee be-tit-kal-LI-mee en-ge-LEE-zee? (TO F.)

137. Does anyone here speak English?
fee ẖahd HE-nah bee-yit-KAL-lim en-ge-LEE-zee?

138. I speak [only] English.
A-nah bat-KAL-lim en-ge-LEE-zee [bass].

139. I know [some] [French].
A-nah BAH-ruff [SHWI̱-yit] [fah-rahn-SA-wee].

140. ——— **German.**
——— al-MA-nee.

141. ——— **Russian.**
——— ROO-see.

142. ——— **Italian.**
——— ee-TAH-lee.

143. ——— **Spanish.**
——— es-BA-nee.

144. Please speak more slowly.
min-FAHD-luk et-KAL-lim AH-lah MAH-lak. (TO M.)
min-FAHD-lik et-kal-LI-mee AH-lah MAH-lik. (TO F.)

145. I understand you.
fe-HEMT.

146. I did not understand.
mahf-HEM-tish.

147. Repeat it, please.
bit-OOL ay min-FAHD-luk. (TO M.)
bit-OO-lee ay min-FAHD-lik. (TO F.)

148. Do you understand me?
fe-hem-TI-nee? (TO M.)
fe-hem-TEE-nee? (TO F.)
fe-hem-TOO-nee? (TO GR.)

149. How do you say "———" in Arabic?
YAH-nee ay " ——— " bil-AH-rah-bee?

150. What does this mean?
YAH-nee ay?

151. I know.
A-nah AH-rif. (M.)
A-nah AHR-fah. (F.)

152. We know.
EH-nah ahr-FEEN.

153. I do not know.
A-nah mish AH-rif. (M.)
A-nah mish AHR-fah. (F.)

154. We do not know.
EH-nah mish ahr-FEEN.

155. I believe so (I think so).
af-TI-ker KE-da.

156. I do not believe (think) so.
MAF-ti-kersh.

157. What is that?
ay da?

158. What do you do with it?
AH-lah shan ay da?

159. How do you go there?
ah-ROOH he-NAK iz-ZI?

160. We need an interpreter.
EH-nah ow-ZEEN mu-TAR-gim.

DIFFICULTIES

161. Where is [the American Embassy]?
fayn [is-se-FAH-rah el-am-ree-KEE-ya]?

162. ———— the police station?
———— IS-me el-boh-LEES (OR ish-SHOR-tah)?

163. ———— the lost and found office?
———— MAK-tab el-a-ma-NAT?

164. ———— the washroom?
———— DOH-rit el-MI-yah?

165. ———— the men's room?
———— mir-ḤAHD ir-re-GAL?

166. ———— the ladies' room?
———— toh-wah-LET is-si-yi-DAT?

167. ———— a physician?
———— tah-BEEB bah-TIN-nee?

168. ———— a clinic?
———— ay-YA-da?

169. ———— a dentist?
———— tah-BEEB is-NAN?

170. Can you [help me] tell me?
TE'-dahr [ti-sah-ED-nee] te-ŪL-lee? (TO M.)
te'-DAH-ree [ti-sah-DEE-nee] (te-oo-LEE-lee)? (TO F.)

171. I am looking for my [boy friend] girl friend.
A-nah bah-DOW-wahr AH-lah [SAḤ-bee] saḥ-BIT-tee.

172. I cannot find the address of the hotel.
mish-LA-ee en-WAHN el-loh-KAHN-dah.
(M.)
mish-LA'-yah en-WAHN el-loh-KAHN-dah.
(F.)

173. She has lost her handbag.
shahn-TET-hah DAH'-et.

174. He has lost his billfold.
maħ-FAHZ-toh DAH'-et.

175. We forgot the keys.
ne-SEE-na el-mah-fah-TEEĦ.

176. They missed the train.
FAT-hom el-AHT-re.

177. It is not my fault.
mish ŕahl-TIT-tee.

178. I do not remember [the name of] the street.
mish FA-ker [IS-me] ish-SHAR-yah.

179. What am I to do [now]?
AH'-mill ay [del-WA'-tee]?

180. Where are we going?
EĦ-nah rī-ĦEEN fayn?

181. Let me alone!
SIB-nee fi-ĦAH-lee! (TO M.)
si-BEE-nee fi-ĦAH-lee! (TO F.)
si-BOO-nee fi-ĦAH-lee! (TO GR.)

182. Help!
el-ḥah-OO-nay!

183. Thief!
ḥah-RAH-may!

184. Fire!
ḥah-REE-ah!

CUSTOMS

185. Where is the customs?
fayn el-GŪM-rūk?

186. Here is [the passport].
[ga-WAZ is-SAH-fahr] ah-HOH.

187. —— the visa.
—— et-ta'-SHEE-ra.

188. —— the identification card.
—— el-be-TAH-ah ish-shakh-SEE-ya.

189. —— the health certificate.
—— ish-sha-HA-da es-se-ḤEE-ya.

190. —— the baggage.
—— el-AHFSH.

191. These suitcases are mine.
ish-SHOH-naht dee be-TAH-tee.

192. I have nothing to declare.
mam-ah-YEESH ḤA-ga ah-LAY-ha GŪM-rūk.

193. **This suitcase contains gifts.**
ish-SHAHN-tah dee FEE-ha ha-DA-ya.

194. **Must I open everything?**
LA-zim AF-taĥ kūll ĤA-ga?

195. **All this is for my personal use.**
kūll dee ĥa-GAT shakh-SEE-ya.

196. **There is nothing in that but clothing.**
ma-FEESH HE-nah ĤA-ga IL-la hoh-DOOM.

197. **That is all I have.**
da kūll IL-lee may-Ĭ-yah.

198. **How much must I pay?**
LA-zim AD-fah kam?

BAGGAGE

199. **Where can I check the baggage?**
a-SAL-lim ish-SHOH-naht fayn?

200. **The baggage room.**
OH-dit el-AHFSH.

201. **The receipt.**
el-WAHS-le.

202. **The number.**
in-NIM-rah.

203. **These suitcases to the [left] [right] belong to me.**
ish-SHOH-naht IL-lee AH-lah [ish-shi-MAL] [el-yi-MEEN] dee be-TAH-tee.

204. I cannot find all my baggage.
mish-LA-ee kūll ish-SHOH-naht be-TAH-
tee. (M.)
mish-LA'-yah kūll ish-SHOH-naht be-TAH-
tee. (F.)

205. Can I leave these things here for a while?
MOHM-kin a-SEEB el-ḥa-GAT dee HE-
nah SHWĪ-yah?

206. I want to leave these bags here [for a few days].
A-nah AII-wiz a-SEEB ish-SHOH-naht dee
HE-nah [kam YOHM]. (M.)
A-nah OW-zah a-SEEB ish-SHOH-naht
dee HE-nah [kam YOHM]. (F.)

207. Porter!
ya-shī-YAL!

208. Please carry these for me.
min-FAHD-luk SHEL-lee dohl. (TO M.)

209. Take me to a taxi.
wahd-DEE-nee lee TAK-si. (TO M.)

210. Follow me, please.
tah-AH-lah wah-RAH-yah min-FAHD-luk.
(TO M.)

211. Handle this very carefully.
ḤAH-sib AH-lah dee. (TO M.)

212. How much do I owe you?
AH-wiz kam? (TO M.)
OW-zah kam? (TO F.)

TRAVEL DIRECTIONS

213. Can you recommend a [good] travel agency?
EN-tah TAH-ruff MAK-tab see-YA-ħee [KWĬ-yis]? (TO M.)
EN-tee tah-RUF-fee MAK-tab see-YA-ħee [KWĬ-yis]? (TO F.)

214. What is the fastest way?
ay AHS-rah tah-REE-ah?

215. I want to go [to the airline office].
A-nah AH-wiz ah-ROOĦ [MAK-tab SHIR-kit it-tah-yah-RAHN]. (M.)
A-nah OW-zah ah-ROOĦ [MAK-tab SHIR-kit it-tah-yah-RAHN]. (F.)

216. —— to the information desk.
—— MAK-tab el-is-tay-la-MAT.

217. —— to the tourist information office.
—— MAK-tab is-see-YA-ħah.

218. Where is [the railroad station]?
fayn [may-ĦAH-tet is-SIK-ka el-ħa-DEED]?

219. —— the bus stop?
—— may-ĦAH-tet el-oh-toh-BEES?

220. ——— **the business section?**
——— wist el-BA-lud?

221. ——— **the shop?**
——— el-mah-ḤAHL?

222. ——— **the suburb?**
——— id-DAḤ-yah?

223. **Is this the direct way to** ———**?**
IIEE-yah dee SIK-ket ———?

224. **Am I going in the right direction?**
A-nah rah-YEḤ fill it-ti-GAH is-SAH-ḥeeḥ?

225. **How long is the trip to the airport?**
el-ma-SA-fa lil mah-TAHR ad-dee-AY?

226. **When will we arrive?**
ḥa-NOO-sull EM-tah?

227. **Please tell me when we arrive.**
min-FAHD-luk ŪL-lee LAM-ma NOO-sull.
   (TO M.)
min-FAHD-lik oo-LEE-lee LAM-ma NOO-sull. (TO F.)

228. **Please show me the way.**
min-FAHD-luk wah-REE-nee is-SIK-ka.
min-FAHD-lik wah-REE-nee is-SIK-ka.

229. **Should I turn [left]?**
LA-zim ah-ḤOW wid [shi-MAL]?

230. ——— **right?**
——— yi-MEEN?

231. —— **south?**
—— ga-NOOB?

232. —— **east?**
—— shar'?

233. —— **west?**
—— r̃ahrb?

234. —— **at the traffic light?**
—— ahnd i-SHAH-ret el-moh-ROOR?

235. —— **at the next corner?**
—— ahnd in-NAHS-yah IL-lee GĬ-ya?

236. —— **at the corner next to the large apartment building?**
—— AH-lah NAHS-yit el-ay-MAH-rah el-ki-BEE-ra?

237. **Is it [on this side of the street]?**
HOO-wah [AH-lah in-NAH̃-ya dee]? (referring to masculine noun)
HEE-yah [AH-lah in-NAH̃-ya dee]? (referring to feminine noun)

238. —— **on the other side?**
—— AH-lah in-NAH̃-ya it-TAN-ya?

239. —— **on the corner?**
—— AH-lah in-NAHS-yah?

240. —— **inside the station?**
—— GOO-wah el-may-H̃AH-tah?

241. —— **in front of the building?**
—— ohd-DAM el-MAB-na?

242. —— **facing the garden?**
—— ohd-DAM el-gi-NAY-na?

243. —— **beside the café?**
—— ganb el-AH-wah?

244. —— **next to the restaurant?**
—— ganb el-maht-AHM?

245. —— **in front of the statue?**
—— ohd-DAM it-tim-SAL?

246. —— **in back?**
—— WAH-rah?

247. —— **behind the school?**
—— WAH-rah el-mad-RA-sa?

248. —— **in the square?**
—— fill-mee-DAN?

249. —— **straight ahead?**
—— AH-lah tool?

250. —— **a little way from the bus stop?**
—— oh-RĪ-yib min may-H̄AH-tet el-oh-
toh-BEES?

251. **Do I have to cross the bridge?**
LA-zim ah-AHD-dee el-KŪB-ree?

252. **Is it [near] far?**
HOO-wah [oh-RĪ-yib] bay-EED? (referring to masculine noun)
HEE yah [oh-ri-YIB-hah] bay-EE-da? (referring to feminine noun)

253. How far is it?
  bay-EED ad-dee-AY? (referring to masculine noun)
  bay-EE-da ad-dee-AY? (referring to feminine noun)

254. How does one get there?
  ah-ROOH̱ he-NAK iz-ZĬ?

255. Can I walk this distance?
  AH'-dahr AM-shee el-ma-SA-fa dee?

256. After how many blocks shall I turn?
  ah-H̱OW-wid bahd kam SHAR-yah?

TICKETS

257. Where is [the ticket office]?
  fayn [shib-BAK it-ta-ZA-ker]?

258. ——— the waiting room?
  ——— OH-det el-in-te-ZAHR?

259. How much is a [round trip] ticket to Alexandria?
  bee-KAM it-tahz-KAH-rah [rah-yeẖ-GĬ] lis-ken-de-REE-yah?

260. Give me a ticket to [Aswan].
  id-DEE-nee tahz-KAH-rah lee [ahs-WAHN].

261. First class [sleeper].
  DAH-rah-gah OO-lah [nohm].

262. Second class.
DAH-rah-gah TAN-ya.

263. Platform ticket.
tahz-KAH-rit moh-AB-la.*

264. A reserved seat.
KŪR-see maḥ-GOOZ.

265. A timetable.
da-LEEL.

266. How long is this ticket good?
it-tahz-KAH-rah dee SAHL-ḥah lee EM-tah?

267. How many valises may I take?
AH'-dahr a-KHŪD kam SHAN-tah?

268. Can I travel by way of [Suez]?
AH'-dahr a-SA-fir ahn tah-REE' [is-SOO-wes]?

269. Can I get something to eat on this trip?
AH'-dahr A-kūll fee is-SIK-ka?

TRAVEL BY PLANE

270. Is there a bus service to the airport?
fee oh-toh-bi-SAT bet-ROOḤ lil mah-TAHR?

* A platform ticket is required in order to get into the platform area when seeing off or meeting someone.

271. At what time does it arrive?
YOO-sull is-SA-a' kam?

272. I have a confirmed reservation.
A-nah may-AH-yah ḤAG-ze.

273. When is there a flight to [Beirut]?
fee tah-YAH-rah EM-tah lee [bī-ROOT]?

274. What is the flight number?
tah-yah-RAHN NIM-rah kam?

275. How many kilos am I allowed?
AH'-dahr a-KHŪD kam KEE-loh?

276. How much per kilo for excess?
bee-KAM el-KEE-loh iz-zee-YA-da?

277. Give me a round trip ticket to [Baghdad].
id-DEE-nee tahz-KAH-rah rah-yeḥ-GĪ lee [bař-DAD.]

278. Is food served on the plane?
fee AK-le fit-tah-YAH-rah?

TRAVEL BY BOAT

279. Bon voyage!
MAH-ah is-sa-LA-ma!

280. Pier.
rah-SEEF el-MEE-na.

281. Dockyard.
tar-SA-na.

282. I want [to rent] a deck chair.
A-nah   AH-wiz   [ah-ŪG-gahr]   KŪR-see
MAR-kib. (M.)

A-nah   OW-zah   [ah-ŪG-gahr]   KŪR-see
MAR-kib. (F.)

283. When does the boat leave?
el-MAR-kib ħat-OOM EM-tah?

284. Can I go ashore at Port Said?
AH'-dahr AN-zill fee boor sa-EED?

285. Open the ventilator, please.
EF-taħ it-tah-WEE-ya min-FAHD-luk. (TO
M.)

ef-TA-ħee   it-tah-WEE-ya   min-FAHD-lik.
(TO F.)

286. Where is the captain?
fayn el-ohb-TAIIN?

287. I am going to the cabin.
A-nah RAH-yeħ el-ka-BEE-nah. (M.)
A-nah RĪ-ħah el-ka-BEE-nah. (F.)

288. I feel seasick.
A-nah AHN-dee dah-WAHR.

289. Have you a remedy for seasickness?
may-AHK DA-wa lid-dah-WAHR? (TO M.)
may-AH-kee DA-wa lid-dah-WAHR? (TO
F.)

290. The lifeboat.
zoh-RA' in-nah-GAH.

291. The life preserver.
toh' in-nah-GAH.

TRAVEL BY TRAIN

292. The railway station.
may-H̄AH-tet is-SIK-ka el-h̄a-DEED.

293. The platform.
ir-rah-SEEF.

294. Arrival.
woo-SOOL.

295. Departure.
ee-YAM.

296. When does the next train for Luxor leave?
el-AH-tre IL-lee RAH-yeh̄ lil LO'-sohr yo-OOM EM-tah?

297. My train leaves in [a quarter of an hour].
el-AH-tre h̄ī-OOM ka-MAN [rob' SA-a'].

298. From what platform does the train leave?
el-AH-tre h̄ī-OOM min AN-hoo rah-SEEF?

299. Does this train stop at [Assiut]?
el-AH-tre da bee-YOO-af fee [ass-YOOT]?

300. How long does the train stop?
el-AH-tre bee-YOO-af ad-dee-AY?

301. Is there an express train to [Cairo]?
fee AH-tre sa-REE-yah lee [MAHS-re]?

302. Is there a [later] [earlier] train?
fee AH-tre [BAH-doh] [AB-loh]?

303. Please [open] [close] the window.
min-FAHD-luk [EF-tah] [E'-fill] ish-shib-
BAK. (TO M.)
min-FAHD-lik [ef-TA-hee] [e'-FIL-lee] ish-
shib-BAK. (TO F.)

304. Where is [the dining car]?
fayn [ah-rah-BEE-yit el-AK-le]?

305. ———— the sleeper?
———— ah-rah-BEE-yit in-NOHM?

306. ———— the baggage car?
———— ah-rah-BEE-yit el-AFSH?

307. ———— the washroom (or bathroom)?
———— DOH-ret el-MI-yah?

308. Is this seat taken?
el-KÜR-see da mah-GOOZ?

309. May I smoke?
AH'-dahr ah-DAKH-ahn?

TRAVEL BY BUS AND
STREETCAR

310. Driver.
sow-WA'.

311. Conductor.
kom-SA-ree.

312. Inspector.
mū-FAT-tish.

313. Where does the streetcar stop?
may-ḤAH-tet it-tohr-MĪ fayn?

314. What bus goes to ——?
oh-toh-BEES NIM-rah kam bay-ROOḤ
——?

315. How much is the fare?
bee-KAM it-tahz-KAH-rah?

**316. After how many stations does it arrive
at ——?**
bahd kam may-ḤAH-tah ḥah-NOO-sull
——?

317. Please, do you go near ——?
min-FAHD-luk, EN-tah bit-ROOḤ oh-
RAH-yib min ——? (TO M.)

318. Will I have to change?
LA-zim ah-ŘĪ-yahr?

319. I want to get off at the next stop.
A-nah AH-wiz AN-zill el-may-ḤAH-tah
IL-lee GA-yah. (M.)
A-nah OW-zah AN-zill el-may-ḤAH-tah
IL-lee GA-yah. (F.)

320. We want to get off here.
EḤ-nah OW-zeen NIN-zill HE-nah.

321. Please tell me where to get off.
min-FAHD-luk ŪL-lee AN-zill fayn. (TO M.)

TRAVEL BY TAXI

322. Please call a cab for me.
min-FAHD-luk na-DEE-lee TAK-si. (TO M. throughout this section)

323. Are you free, [driver]?
EN-tah FAH-dee [YAHS-tah OR ya sow-WA']?

324. What do you charge [per hour] per kilometer?
el-OHG-rah kam [fee is-SA-a'] fill KEE-loh?

325. How much will the ride cost?
TA-khūd kam fir-REĦ-la?

326. Drive us around for one hour.
soo' BEE-nah SA-a'.

327. Please drive more slowly.
min-FAHD-luk soo' AH-lah MAH-lak.

328. Can you stop here?
TE'-dahr TOH-af HE-nah?

329. Please wait for me here.
min-FAHD-luk is-tan NA-nee HE-nah.

330. How much do I owe you?
AH-wiz kam?

TRAVEL BY AUTOMOBILE*

331. Where can I rent [a car]?
AH'-dahr ah-ŪG-gahr [ah-rah-BEE-ya] fayn?

332. —— a motorcycle?
—— moh-toh-SIK-le?

333. —— a bicycle?
—— AH-gah-lah?

334. I have an international driver's license.
may-AH-yah ROKH-sah dow-LEE-ya.

335. What is the name of [this city (or town or village)]?
is-MA-hah ay [el-BA-lud dee]?

336. —— this suburb?
—— id-DAH̄-yah dee?

337. What is the next town?
ay el-BA-lud IL-lee GĪ-yah?

338. Where does this road lead?
is-SIK-kah dee tee-WAH-dee AH-lah fayn?

339. Is the road paved?
HOO-wah ish-SHAR-yah as-FALT?

340. Can you show it to me on the map?
TE'-dahr tee-wah-REE-nee AH-lah el-kha-REE-tah? (TO M.)
te'-DAH-ree tee-wah-REE-nee AH-lah el-kha-REE-tah? (TO F.)

* See also the road signs facing page 186.

341. Where can I find a gas station?
fee may-ḤAH-tet ban-ZEEN HE-nah?

342. The tank is [empty] full.
it-TANK [FAH-dee] mal-YAN.

343. How much does a liter of gasoline cost?
bee-KAM LIT-re el-ban-ZEEN?

344. Give me twenty liters.
id-DEE-nee ish-REEN LIT-re.

345. Please [change] [check] the oil.
min-FAHD-luk [ḠĪ-yer] [EK-shif AH-lah]
iz-ZAYT. (то м., as in the remainder of
this section)

346. Light, medium, heavy [oil].
[zayt] kha-FEEF, AH-dee, tee-EEL.

347. Put water in the battery.
ḥūt MĪ-yah fill but-tah-REE yah

348. Charge the battery.
ish-ḤEN el-but-tah-REE-yah.

349. Lubricate the car.
SHAḤ-ḥahm el-ah-rah-BEE-ya.

350. Clean the windshield.
NUD-duff el-ee-ZAZ.

351. Could you wash it [now]?
TE'-dahr teḡ-SIL-hah [del-WAʼ-tee]?

352. May I park here [for a while]?
AHʼ-dahr AR-kin el-ah-rah-BEE-ya HE-
nah [SHWĪ-yah]?

353. Can I leave the car here [overnight]?
    AH'-dahr a-SEEB el-ah-rah-BEE-ya HE-
      nah [el-lay-LA-dee]?

354. Can you recommend a good mechanic?
    TE'-dahr ti-dil-LI-nee AH-lah me-ka-NEE-
      kee KWĪ-yis?

355. Adjust the brakes.
    OZ-bot el-fah-RAH-mill.

356. Check the tires.
    EK-shif AH-lah el-AH-gull.

357. Can you repair this tire?
    TE'-dahr te-SAHL-laĥ el-AH-gah-lah dee?

358. The motor overheats.
    el-moh-TOHR bee-YIS-khun.

359. The engine misses.
    el-moh-TOHR bay-FOW-wit.

360. The engine squeaks.
    el-moh-TOHR bee-YIZ-ah'.

361. The car does not go.
    el-ah-rah-BEE-ya aht-LAH-nah.

HELP ON THE ROAD

362. I am sorry to trouble you.
    A-nah A-sif lim-dī-AY-tak. (M. TO M.)
    A-nah AS-fah lim-dī-AY-tak. (F. TO M.)

363. My car has broken down.
ah-rah-BEE-tee ET-let.

364. Will you help me push the car to the side, please?
TE'-dahr ti-sa-ID-nee fee za' el-ah-rah-BEE-ya min-FAHD-luk? (TO M.)

365. Would you push me, please?
ZA'-ah ya-AHM min-FAHD-luk? (TO M.)
ZA'-ah ya-gah-MAH-ah min-fahd-LOH-kūm? (TO GR.)

366. Can you lend me a jack?
MOHM-kin ti-sal-LIF-nee el-af-REE-ta? (TO M.)

367. Will you help me put on the spare tire?
TE'-dahr ti-sa-ID-nee fee tar-KEEB lis-TIB-ne? (TO M.)

368. My car is stuck [in the mud].
ah-rah-BEE-tee ṚA-ra-zit [fit-TEEN].

369. My car is lying in the ditch.
ah-rah-BEE-tee WE'-et fill ḤOF-rah.

370. Could you drive me to the nearest gas station, please?
MOHM-kim ti-wah-SUL-nee lim-ḤAH-tet ban-ZEEN min-FAHD-luk? (TO M.)

PARTS OF THE CAR

371. Accelerator (gas pedal).
be-DAL el-ban-ZEEN.

372. Battery.
but-tah-REE-yah.

373. Brakes.
fah-RAH-mil.

374. Hand brakes.
fahr-MAH-lit el-EED.

375. Clutch.
dib-ree-YASH.

376. Crank.
ma-na-FIL-la.

377. Engine.
moh-TOHR.

378. Gear shift.
fi-TAYS.

379. Lights.
noor.

380. Headlights.
noor od-da-MA-nee.

381. Taillights.
noor wahr-RAH-nee.

382. Horn.
ka-LAKS.

383. Spark plugs.
boh-jay-HAT.

384. Steering wheel.
dee-rik-see-YOHN.

385. Tire.
AH-gah-lah.

386. Front tires.
AH-gah-lah od-da-ma-NEE-yah.

387. Rear tires.
AH-gah-lah wahr-rah-NEE-yah.

388. Spare tires.
AH-gah-lah STIB-ne.

389. Radiator.
ra-dee-ya-TAYR.

390. Windshield.
bah-rah-BREEZ.

391. Windshield wipers.
mas-sa-ḤAHT.

TOOLS AND EQUIPMENT

392. Chain.
sil-SI-la.

393. Hammer.
sha-KOOSH.

394. Lever.
A-ga-na.

395. Nail.
mohs-MAHR.

396. Pointed pliers.
zahr-rah-DEE-yah.

397. **Flat-ended pliers.**
kam-MA-shah.

398. **Rope.**
ḤAB-le.

399. **Saw.**
mohn-SHAHR.

400. **Screw.**
ah-lah-WOHZ.

401. **Screwdriver.**
mi-FAK.

402. **Tire pump.**
mohn-FAKH.

403. **Wrench.**
mohf-TAḤ en-ge-LEE-zee.

MAIL

404. **Where is [the post office]?**
fayn [el-BOHS-tah]?

405. ——— **a letter box?**
——— san-DOO' el-BOHS-tah?

406. **To which window should I go?**
ah-ROOḤ lee-AN-hoo shib-BAK?

407. **I want to send this [by surface mail].**
A-nah AH-wiz AB-aht dee [bill ba-REED
el-AH-dee]. (M.)
A-nah OW-zah AB-aht dee [bill ba-REED
el-AH-dee]. (F.)

408. —— **air mail.**
—— ba-REED GOW-wee.

409. —— **special delivery.**
—— ba-REED mis-TA-gill.

410. —— **registered mail.**
—— ba-REED moo-SAG-gull.

411. —— **parcel post.**
—— TAHR-de.

412. **This is only printed matter.**
dee kūl-LAH-hah maht-boo-AHT.

413. **With insurance, please.**
am-MIN-hah min-FAHD-luk.

414. **Will it go out [today]?**
haht-ROOH [in-nay-HAHR-dah]?

415. **Please give me two nine-piaster stamps.**
tah-bee-AYN bee-TES-ah saŕ el-WAH-hed
min-FAHD-luk.

416. **I want to send a money order.**
A-nah AH-wiz AB-aht hay-WA-lah ba-ree-
DEE-yah. (M.)
A-nah OW-zah AB-aht hay-WA-lah ba-ree-
DEE-yah. (F.)

TELEGRAM

417. **I would like to send a telegram.**
A-nah AH-wiz AB-aht tel-leŕ-RAHF. (M.)
A-nah OW-zah AB-aht tel-leŕ-RAIIF. (F.)

418. What is the word rate to Boston [America]?

bee-KAM el-KILL-ma lee BOS-ton [am-REE-ka]?

419. For how many words?

lee-KAM KILL-mah?

420. How much will it cost?

ḤAH-tet KAL-liff kam?

421. When will it arrive?

ḥah-TOO-sull EM-tah?

TELEPHONE

422. May I use the telephone, please?

AH'-dahr as-TA-mill it-te-le-FOHN min-FAHD-luk? (TO M.)

423. Will you dial this number for me, please?

TE'-dahr tet-LOB-lee in-NIM-rah dee min-FAHD-luk? (TO M.)

te'-DAH-ree tet-loh-BEE-lee in-NIM-rah dee min-FAHD-lik? (TO F.)

424. Will you call me at this number?

TE'-dahr tet-LOB-nee fin-NIM-rah dee min-FAHD-luk? (TO M.)

te'-DAH-ree tet-loh-BEE-nee fin-NIM-rah dee min-FAHD-lik? (TO F.)

425. I want to make a call to this number.
A-nah AH-wiz AHT-lohb in-NIM-rah dee.
(M.)

A-nah OW-zah AHT-lohb in-NIM-rah dee.
(F.)

426. My telephone number is ———.
NIM-ret te-le-FOH-nee ———.

427. How much is a long-distance call to [Damascus]?
bee-KAM el-moh-KAL-mah el-kha-ri-GEE-yah lee [dee-MASH']?

428. Hello (on the telephone).
ah-LOH.

429. They do not answer.
mah-ḤAHD-dish bee-ROD.

430. The line is busy.
in-NIM-rah mash-ṘOO-la.

431. This is ——— speaking.
A-nah ———.

432. Please hold the line.
khal-LEEK may-Ī-yah min-FAHD-luk. (TO M.)

khal-LEE-kee may-Ī-yah min-FAHD-lik. (TO F.)

433. He is not here.
mish mow-GOOD.

434. May I leave a message?
AH'-dahr a-SEEB ree-SA-la?

435. I shall call back later.
ḤAHT-lohb TA-nee.

436. You are wanted on the telephone.
fee te-le-FOHN AH-lah SHA-nak. (TO M.)
fee te-le-FOHN AH-lah SHA-nik. (TO F.)

HOTEL

437. I am looking for [a good hotel].
A-nah bah-DOW-wahr AH-lah [loh-KAHN-
dah kwī-YIS-sa].

438. —— the best hotel.
—— AḤ-san loh-KAHN-dah.

439. —— a boarding house.
—— ban-see-YOHN.

440. —— an inexpensive hotel.
—— loh-KAHN-dah re-KHEE-sah.

441. I want to be in the center of town.
A-nah AH-wiz a-KOON fee wist el-BA-lud.
(M.)
A-nah OW-zah a-KOON fee wist el-BA-lud.
(F.)

**442. I would prefer to be (LIT.: Better)
close to [the University].**
AḤ-san oh-RĪ-yib min [el-GAHM-ah].

443. —— the American Embassy.
—— is-se-FAH-rah el-am-ree-KEE-ya.

444. —— **the Nile.**
—— in-NEEL.

445. I have a reservation for tonight.
A-nah ḤA-giz el-lay-LA-dee. (M.)
A-nah ḤAG-za el-lay-LA-dee. (F.)

446. Do you have [a room]?
fee [OH-dah] FAHD-yah?

447. —— **a double room?**
—— OH-dah lit-NAYN?

448. —— **an air-conditioned room?**
—— OH-dah moo-kī-YA-fa?

449. —— **a suite?**
—— ge-NAḤ?

450. I want a room.
A-nah AH-wiz OH-dah. (M.)
A-nah OW-zah OH-dah. (F.)

451. —— **with a double bed.**
—— bis-REER DŪB-le.

452. —— **with twin beds.**
—— bis-ree-RAYN.

453. —— **with a bath.**
—— bee ḥahm-MAM.

454. —— **with a shower.**
—— bee dūsh.

455. —— **with running water.**
—— bee ḥohd.

456. ——— **with hot water.**
——— bee MÍ-yah SOKH-nah.

457. ——— **with a balcony.**
——— bee ba-la-KOH-nah.

458. ——— **with a radio.**
——— bee RAH-dee-yoh.

459. ——— **with a telephone.**
——— bee te-le-FOHN.

460. ——— **with a television.**
——— bee te-le-viz-YOHN.

461. I shall take a room [for one night].
id-DEE-nee OH-dah [li-LAY-lah WAH̄-dah].

462. ——— **for a week or so.**
——— h̄ah-WAH-lee ohs-BOO'.

463. ——— **for two persons.**
——— lee nah-fah-RAYN.

464. Can I have it [with meals]?
AH'-dahr a-KHŪD-hah [bill-AK-le]?

465. ——— **without meals?**
——— min-R̄AY-re AK-le?

466. ——— **with breakfast [only]?**
——— bil-foh-TAHR [bass]?

467. What is the rate [per night]?
bee-KAM [el-LAY-lah]?

468. ——— **per week?**
——— el ohs-BOO'?

469. ——— **per month?**
——— ish-SHAH-re?

470. Are tax and room service included?
id-dah-REE-bah will-KHID-mah maĥ-soo-
BEEN?

471. I should like to see the room.
AH'-dahr a-SHOOF el-OH-dah?

472. Have you something [better]?
AN-dak ĤA-ga [AĤ-san]? (TO. M.)
AN-dik ĤA-ga [AĤ-san]? (TO F.)

473. ——— **cheaper?**
——— AHR-khahs?

474. ——— **larger?**
——— AHK-bahr?

475. ——— **smaller?**
——— AHS-ŕahr.

476. ——— **on a [lower] [higher] floor?**
——— fee-DOHR [OW-tah] [AH-lah]?

477. ——— **with more light?**
——— bee noor AK-tahr?

478. ——— **with more air?**
——— bee ta-WEE-yah AĤ-san?

479. ——— **upstairs?**
——— foh'?

480. ——— **downstairs?**
——— taĥt?

481. Is there an elevator?
fee ah-sun-SAYR?

482. What is my room number?
NIM-ret el-OH-dah kam?

483. My room key, please.
mohf-TAH el-OH-dah min-FAHD-luk. (TO
M.)

484. Please wake me at eight in the morning.
min-FAHD-luk sah-HEE-nee is-SA-a' ta-
MAN-ya is-SOB-he. (TO M.)

485. I want my breakfast in my room.
A-nah AH-wiz el-foh-TAHR fill-OH-dah.
(M.)
A-nah OW-zah el-foh-TAHR fill-OH-dah.
(F.)

486. I want (to speak to) the manager.
A-nah AH-wiz el-moo-DEER (MASC.) [el-
moo-DEER-ra (FEM.)]. (M.)
A-nah OW-zah el-moo-DEER (MASC.) [el-
moo-DEER-ra (FEM.)]. (F.)

487. Have you [a letter] for me?
AN-dak [gah-WAB] LEE-yah? (TO M.)
AN-dik [gah-WAB] LEE-yah? (TO F.)

488. ——— a message?
——— ree-SA-la?

489. ——— a parcel?
——— TAHR-de?

490. Please forward my mail to ———.
min-FAHD-luk EB-aht el-BOS-tah be-TAH-
tee lee ———. (TO M.)

491. Please send a [chambermaid].
min-FAHD-luk eb-AHT-lee [khad-DA-ma].
(TO M.)

492. ——— valet.
——— khad-DAM.

493. ——— waiter.
——— gahr-SOHN.

494. ——— porter.
——— shī-YAL.

495. ——— messenger.
——— moo-RAS-lah.

496. I am expecting [a friend of mine].
A-nah mis-TAN-nee [WAH-ħed SAĦ-bee
(MASC.); WAH-dah saħ-BI-tee (FEM.)].
(M.)
A-nah mis-tan-NEE-yah [WAH-ħed SAĦ-
bee (MASC.); WAH-dah saħ-BI-tee (FEM.)].
(F.)

497. ——— a telephone call.
——— te le-FOHN.

498. Can I leave these valuables in the hotel safe?
AH'-dahr a-SEEB el-ħa-GAT dee fill a-ma-
NAT?

499. I would like to get the money from the safe.
    A-nah AH-wiz el-fe-LOOS min el-a-ma-NAT. (M.)
    A-nah OW-zah el-fe-LOOS min el-a-ma-NAT. (F.)

500. I would like to get my [jewelry] back.
    A-nah OW-zah [el-ga-WA-hir] be-TAH-tee TA-nee. (F.)

501. When must I check out?
    a-SEEB el-OH-dah EM-tah?

CHAMBERMAID*

502. The door doesn't lock.
    el-BAB ma-bee-YE'-filsh.

503. The room is too [cold] hot.
    el-OH-dah [bard] ḥahr.

504. This shirt is for washing [and ironing].
    el-ah-MEES da lil-ḟah-SEEL [wil-MAK-wa].

505. This [suit] is for dry cleaning.
    [ed-BAD-la] dee lit-tan-toor-LAY.

506. Please bring me [another blanket].
    min-FAHD-lik ha-TEE-lee [but-tah-NEE-ya TAN-ya].

---

* Naturally, the sentences in this section are addressed to a female.

507. ——— **coathangers.**
——— sham-ma-AHT.

508. ——— **a glass.**
——— kūb-BA-ya.

509. ——— **a pillow.**
——— may-KHUD-da.

510. ——— **a bed sheet.**
——— mee-LA-ya.

511. ——— **soap.**
——— sah-BOON.

512. ——— **toilet paper.**
——— WA-ra' toh-wah-LET.

513. ——— **towel.**
——— FOO-tah.

**514. Please do not disturb me until ———
o'clock.**
min-FAHD-lik si-BEE-nee a-NAM les-SA-a'
———.

515. Please change the sheets.
min-FAHD-lik rī-YA-ree el-mi-la-YAT.

516. Please make the bed.
min-FAHD-lik rut-TI-bee is-se-REER.

517. Please come back later.
min-FAHD-lik ta-AH-lee ka-MAN SHWĬ-
yah.

APARTMENT

518. I am looking for [a furnished] [an unfurnished] apartment.
A-nah bah-DOW-wahr AH-lah SHA'-ah [muf-ROO-sha] [FAHD-yah].

519. —— with bathroom.
—— bee DOH-rit MĪ-yah.

520. —— with two bedrooms.
—— bee od-TAYN nohm.

521. —— with a reception room.
—— bee OH-dit gū-LOOS (OR sah-LOHN).

522. —— with a living room.
—— bee SAH-lah.

523. —— with a dining room.
—— bee OH-dit SOHF-rah.

524. —— with a kitchen.
—— bee MUT-bakh.

525. Do you furnish [the linen]?
bill [mi-la-YAT]?

526. —— the dishes [china]?
—— et-BAH' [SAY-nee]?

527. —— the servant?
—— khad-DAM? (MASC.)
—— khad-DA-ma? (FEM.)

528. Can you recommend a good cook?
TE'-dahr ti-dil-LI-nee AH-lah tub-BAHKH
KWĪ-yis (MASC.) [tub-BAH-khah kwī-
YIS-sa (FEM.)]? (TO M.)
te'-DAH-ree ti-dil-LEE-nee AH-lah tub-
BAHKH KWĪ-yis (MASC.) [tub-BAH-khah
kwī-YIS-sa (FEM.)]? (TO F.)

CAFÉ

529. I'd like to have [a coffee].
id-DEE-nee [WAH-ħed AH-wah].

530. —— a tea.
—— WAH-ħed shī.

531. —— an orange soda.
—— WAH-ħed bohr-too-AN.

532. —— a lemonade.
—— WAH-ħed lah-MOON.

533. —— a beer.
—— BEE-ra.*

RESTAURANT

534. Is there a good restaurant in this area?
fee ĦE-nah MAHT-ahm KWĪ-yis?

* Alcoholic beverages can be ordered in bars and hotels
only; you may use the English words for any drink.

535. Breakfast.
foh-TAHR.

536. Dinner (in the early afternoon).
ŘA-da.

537. Supper (night meal).
AH-sha.

538. Sandwich.
san-da-WITSH.

539. Can we have the midday meal now?
NE'-dahr nit-ŘUD-da del-WAH'-tee?

540. Waiter!
gahr-SOHN!

541. We need a table [near the window].
EĦ-nah ow-ZEEN tah-rah-BEE-zah [oh-rī-YI-ba min ish-shib-BAK].

542. —— for four persons.
—— LUR-bah tin-FAHR.

543. —— outside.
—— BUR-rah.

544. —— inside.
—— GOH-wah.

545. —— in the corner.
—— fir-ROHK-ne.

546. What is the specialty of the house?
ay AK-lit-kūm el-mahkh-SOO-sah?

547. Please serve us quickly!
bee SOHR-ah min-FAHD-luk! (TO M.)
bee SOHR-ah min-FAHD-lik! (TO F.)

548. Please bring me [the menu].
[el-LIS-ta] min-FAHD-luk. (TO M.)
[el-LIS-ta] min-FΛHD-lik. (TO F.)

549. ——— bread.
——— aysh.

550. ——— butter.
——— ZIB-da.

551. ——— a fork.
——— SHOH-ka.

552. ——— a knife.
——— sik-KEE-na.

553. ——— a teaspoon.
——— mah-LA-a' soo-rī-YAH-rah.

554. ——— a large spoon.
——— mah-LΛ-a' ki-BEE-ra.

555. ——— a napkin.
——— FOO-tah.

556. ——— a plate.
——— TΛH-hah'.

557. ——— a glass.
——— kūb-BA-ya.

558. I would like to have [a little more] of this, please.
A-nah AH-wiz [ka-MAN SHWĬ-yah] min da* min-FAHD-luk. (M. TO M.)
A-nah AH-wiz [ka-MAN SHWĬ-yah] min da min-FAHD-lik. (M. TO F.)
A-nah OW-zah [ka-MAN SHWĬ-yah] min da min FAHD-luk. (F. TO M.)
A-nah OW-zah [ka-MAN SHWĬ-yah] min da min-FAHD-lik. (F. TO F.)

559. ——— a little less.
——— a-ULL SHWĬ-yah.

560. I like the meat [rare].
A-nah ba-ḤEBB el-LAḤ-mah [nohs SEE-wa].

561. ——— well done.
——— mis-te-WEE-ya KWĬ-yis.

562. ——— boiled.
——— mas-LOO-a.

563. ——— fried.
——— ma'-LEE-ya.

564. ——— roasted.
——— may-ḥahm-MAH-rah.

565. ——— grilled.
——— mash-WEE-ya.

* *Dee* if the "this" referred to is feminine.

566. This meat is [undercooked] burned.
el-LAH̄-mah dee [NI-ya] mah̄-ROO-a.

567. Not too [sweet].
mish [H̄EL-we; H̄EL-wa]*

568. ——— sour.
——— mūrr; mūr-RAH.

569. ——— fat.
——— see-MEEN; see-MEE-na.

570. ——— tough.
——— GA-mid; GAM-da.

571. ——— dry.
——— NA-shiff; NASH-fa.

572. Not too spicy.
ba-LASH boo-hah-RΛHT ke-TEER.

573. This is cold.
da BA-rid (referring to masculine noun).
dee BAR-da (referring to feminine noun).

574. I did not order this.
A-nah ma-tah-LUB-tish da.†

575. Could you give me a salad instead?
TE'-dahr tid-DEE-nee SAH-lah-tah ba-
DAL da?† (TO M.)
te'-DAH-ree tid-DEE-nee SAH-lah-tah ba
DAL da?† (TO F.)

* In sentences 567–571, the first form of the adjective given
is masculine, the second feminine.

† *Dee* if the "this" referred to is feminine.

576. The check, please!
el-ħe-SAB min-FAHD-luk! (TO M.)
el-ħe-SAB min-FAHD-lik! (TO F.)

577. Are the tax and service charge included?
id-dah-REE-bah wil-KHID-mah maħ-soo-BEEN?

578. There is a mistake in the bill.
fee ŔUL-tah fill ħe-SAB.

579. The food was excellent.
el-AK-le kan mom-TAZ.

580. Keep the change.
KHAL-lee el-BA'-ee AH-lah SHA-nuk. (TO M.)
KHAL-lee el-BA'-ee AH-lah SHA-nik. (TO F.)

581. Hearty appetite!
bill HA-na!*

FOOD LIST

582. Drinking water.
MĬ-yet shūrb.

---

* It is also customary to say *ha-NEE-an* to someone after the meal. The meaning conveyed is: "I hope the meal was satisfactory and pleasant and will be nutritive and healthy." The reply is *ahl-LAH yee-hun-NEEK* (TO M.) or *ahl-LAH yee-hun-NEE-kee* (TO F.), which would convey: "May God bring you happiness for wishing me this!" The same expressions are used when one finishes drinking something like a glass of water.

583. Mineral water.
MĬ-yah mah-da-NEE-ya.

584. Sugar.
SŬK-karr.

585. Sugar cane.
AH-sub.

586. Salt.
MAL-ħe.

587. Pepper.
FILL-fill.

588. Sauce.
SUL-sah.

589. Oil.
zayt.

590. Vinegar.
khull.

591. Lime.
lah-MOON.

592. Lemon.
lah-MOON ah-DUL-yah.

593. Mustard.
mŭs-TUR-dah.

594. Onion.
BAH-sull.

595. Garlic.
tohm.

BREAKFAST FOODS

596. Fruit juice.
ah-SEER fa-WA-keh.

597. Orange juice.
ah-SEER bohr-too-AN.

598. Tomato juice.
ah-SEER tah-MAH-tem.

599. Grape juice.
ah-SEER AY-nub.

600. Jam.
moh-RUB-bah.

601. White bread.
aysh FEE-noh.

602. Local bread.
aysh BA-la-dee.

603. Omelette.
EG-gah.

604. Boiled eggs.
bayd mas-LOO'.

605. Fried eggs.
bayd MA'-lee.

606. Beans.
fool.*

* A special type of beans, with a high protein content, grows in Egypt and is served as a breakfast dish, as well as in snack sandwiches. This *fool* (the beans themselves), when ground, spiced and fried is called *tah-MEE-ya* or *fa-LA-fill*.

APPETIZERS AND HORS D'ŒUVRES

607. Soup.
SHOR-bah.

> **608. Vegetable soup.**
> SHOR-bet khoh-DAHR.

> **609. Chicken soup.**
> SHOR-bet ſe-RAKH.

> **610. Tomato soup.**
> SHOR-bet tah-MAH-tem.

> **611. Lentil soup.**
> SHOR-bet ahds.

> **612. Beef broth.**
> SHOR-bet LAH̄-mah.

> **613. "Green soup."**
> moh-loh-KHEE-ya.

614. Salad.
SAH-lah-tah.

> **615. Green salad.**
> SAH-lah-tah KHUD-rah.

> **616. Tomato salad.**
> sah-lah-TET tah-MAH-tem.

> **617. Potato salad.**
> sah-lah-TET bah-TAH-tis.

> **618. Egg salad.**
> sah-lah-TET bayd.

619. Dip.
r̄ah-MOOS.

> **620. Sesame salad.**
> sah-lah-TET tay-H̄EE-nah.

> **621. Eggplant dip.**
> bah-bah r̄ahn-NOOJ.

> **622. Lebanese salad.**
> tub-BOO-la.

> **623. Chick-pea dip.**
> H̄OM-mos.

RICE, MACARONI AND CHEESES

624. Rice.
rūz.

> **625. White rice.**
> rūz AHB-yahd.

> **626. Red rice.**
> rūz AH̄-mahr.

> **627. Rice with vermicelli.**
> rūz bish-shay-REE-yah.

> **628. Rice pudding.**
> rūz bil-LA-bun.

629. Macaroni.
mah-kah-ROH-nah.

630. Shell macaroni.
mah-kah-ROH-nah.

631. Spaghetti.
mah-kah-ROH-nah "spaghetti."

632. Baked macaroni.
mah-kah-ROH-nah bill FOHR-ne.

633. Macaroni with ground beef.
mah-kah-ROH-nah bill LAH-mah el-muf-ROO-mah.

634. Macaroni with tomato sauce.
mah-kah-ROH-nah bis-SUL-sah.

635. Cheese.
GIB-nah.

636. White cheese.
GIB-nah BAY-dah.

637. Romano cheese.
GIB-nah ROO-mee.

638. Chester cheese.
GIB-nah "Chester."

639. Edam or Port Salut.
GIB-nah fa-la-MANK.

MEAT AND POULTRY

640. Lamb.
OO-zee.

641. Mutton.
DAH-nee.

642. Veal.
be-TEL-loh.

643. Breaded veal cutlet.
ska-LOHP pah-NAY.

644. Beef.
ug-GA-lee.

645. Roast beef.
rūz-BEEF.

646. Ham.
jambon (pronounced as in French).

647. Sausage.
so-GO'.

648. Brains.
mohkh.

649. Liver.
KEB-da.

650. Heart.
alb.

651. Deer.
ṛa-ZAL.

652. Shish kebab.
ka-BAB.

653. Chicken.
FAR-kha. (SING.)
fee-RAKH. (PL.)

654. Duck.
BUT-ta. (SING.)
but. (PL.)

655. Goose.
WEZ-za. (SING.)
wizz. (PL.)

656. Turkey.
deek ROO-mee. (SING.)
dee-YOOK ROO-mee. (PL.)

657. Pigeon.
ħa-MΛ-ma. (SING.)
ħa-MAM. (PL.)

SEAFOOD

658. Oysters.
gan-DOF-lee.

659. Crab.
ka-BOOR-ya.

660. Shrimp.
gam-BA-ree.

661. Lobster.
es-ta-KOH-za.

662. Sole.
SA-muk MOO-sa (LIT.: Moses' fish).

663. Porgy.
BOLL-tee (large).
shah-BΛHR (small).

664. Sardine.
sar-DEEN.

665. Salmon.
SA-la-mon.

666. Tuna.
TOO-na.

VEGETABLES

667. Artichokes.
khar-SHOOF.

668. Green beans.
fah-SŪL-ya.

669. Cabbage.
KROM-be.

670. Carrots.
GAH-zahr.

671. Cauliflower.
ahr-nah-BEET.

672. Cucumbers.
khee-YAHR.

673. Okra.
BAM-ya.

674. Peas.
be-SIL-la.

675. Peppers (green).
FILL-fill AHKH-dahr.

676. Potatoes.
bah-TAH-tis.

> **677. Boiled potatoes.**
> bah-TAH-tis mus-LOO-ah.

> **678. Fried potatoes.**
> bah-TAH-tis ma'-LEE-ya.

> **679. Stuffed potatoes.**
> bah-TAH-tis maḥ-SHEE-ya.

FRUITS

680. Apple.
tof-FAḤ.

681. Apricot.
MISH-mish.

682. Banana.
mohz.

> **683. Local banana.**
> mohz BA-la-dee.

> **684. Speckled banana.**
> mohz be-NO'-tah.

685. Raspberries.
toot.

686. Strawberries.
fah-ROW-lah.

687. Grapefruit.
Grapefruit (pronounced as in English).

688. Tangerine.
YOO-sef ah-FAN-dee.

689. Oranges.
bohr-too-AN.

> **690. Large navel oranges.**
> bohr-too-AN be-SŪR-rah.

> **691. Small juicy oranges.**
> bohr-too-AN BA-la-dee.

> **692. Pink oranges.**
> bohr-too-AN be-DUM-moh.

> **693. Extra sweet oranges.**
> bohr-too-AN sūk-KA-ree.

694. Cherries.
krayz.

695. Dates.
BA-laĥ.

> **696. Red dates.**
> BA-laĥ AĤ-mahr.

> **697. Ripe dates.**
> BA-laĥ ROH-tub.

> **698. Tender red dates.**
> BA-laĥ zaĥř-LOOL.

> **699. Yellow dates.**
> BA-laĥ am-HAT.

> **700. Dried dates.**
> BA-laĥ ib-REE-mee.

701. Figs.
teen.

702. Grapes.
AY-nub.

    703. Seedless grapes.
    AY-nub ba-NA-tee.

    704. Green grapes.
    AY-nub fī-YOO-mee.

    705. Long "ladyfinger" grapes.
    AY-nub biz.

    706. Fragrant grapes.
    AY-nub be-REE-ħah.

    707. Purple grapes.
    AY-nub mi-LOO-kee (LIT.: royal grapes).

708. Mango.
MAN-ga.

709. Melon (round watermelon).
but-TEEKH.

    710. Local melon.
    but-TEEKH BA-la-dee.

    711. Sweet melon.
    but-TEEKH SHILL-yan.

    712. Crisp melon.
    but-TEEKH sul-ĦAH-wee.

713. Long melon.
but-TEEKH NIM-se.

714. Long cantaloupe.
shum-MAM.

715. Round cantaloupe.
a-BOON.

716. Peach.
khohkh.

717. Pineapple.
a-na-NAS.

718. Plum.
bar-OO'.

DESSERTS AND NUTS

719. French pastry.
ga-TOH.

720. Cake.
TOHR-tah.

721. Ice cream.
is kraym.

722. Vanilla.
"vanilla."

723. Chocolate.
sho-kah-LAH-tah.

724. Strawberry.
fah-ROW-lah.

725. Pistachio.
FOZ-do'.

726. Pudding (custard).
kraym kah-rah-MELL.

727. Vanilla pudding.
me-hal-la-BEE-ya.

728. Starch pudding.
bah-LOO-zah.

729. Baklava.
ba'-LA-wa.

730. Almonds.
lohz.

731. Hazelnuts.
BON-do'.

732. Peanuts.
fool soo-DA-nee.

733. Walnuts.
gohz.

BEVERAGES

734. Coffee.
AH-wah.

735. Black coffee.
AH-wah SA-da.

736. Black coffee with some sugar.
AH-wah SŪK-karr kha-FEEF.

737. Black coffee with sugar.
AH-wah SŪK-karr muz-BOOT.

738. Black coffee with much sugar.
AH-wah SŪK-karr zee-YA-da.

739. Coffee with cream.
AH-wah bil-LA-bun.

740. Lemonade (home-made).
la-moh-NA-ta.

741. Tea.
shī.

742. Hot tea.
shī.

743. Iced tea.
shī me-TAL-lig.

744. Tea with milk.
shī bil-LA-bun.

745. Tea with mint.
shī bin-nay-NA'.

746. Hot chocolate.
ka-KOW bil-LA-bun.

SIGHTSEEING

747. How can one go to ———?
iz-ZĪ el-WAH-ħed yi-ROOħ ———?

748. Where can I rent [a car]?
AH'-dahr   ah-UG-gahr   [ah-rah-BEE-ya]
fayn?

749. ———— a bicycle?
———— AH-gah-lah?

750. ———— a rowboat?
———— MAR-kib?

751. ———— a sailboat?
———— MAR-kib she-RAH-ee?

752. I want a licensed guide who speaks English.
A-nah ĀH-wiz tŭr-goh-MAN bee-yit-KAL-lim en-ge-LEE-zee. (M.)
A-nah OW-zah tŭr-goh-MAN bee-yit-KAL-lim en-ge-LEE-zee. (F.)

753. We want a licensed guide who speaks English.
EĤ-nah ow-ZEEN tŭr-goh-MAN bee-yit-KAL-lim en-ge-LEE-zee.

754. What is the charge [per hour] per day?
bee-KAM [is-SA-a'] el-YOHM?

755. What is the charge for a trip [to the island]?
bee-KAM ir-REĤ-la [lil-ge-ZEE-ra]?

756. ———— to the mountain?
———— lil-GA-bal?

757. ———— to the sea?
———— lil-BAĤ-re?

758. ——— on the Nile?
——— ahn-NEEL?

759. Call for me tomorrow at my hotel at 8 A.M.
kal-LIM-nee fil-loh-KAHN-dah BOK-rah is-SA-a' ta-MAN-ya is-SOB-ħe. (TO M.)

760. Please show me the sights of interest.
min-FAHD-luk wahr-REE-nee el-a-MA-kin el-moo-HIM-mah. (TO M.)

761. I am interested in [architecture].
A-nah eh-tee-MA-mee fee [el-ee-MAH-rah].

762. ——— sculpture.
——— in-NĀĦT.

763. ——— paintings.
——— ir-RAS-me.

764. ——— calligraphy.
——— il-khoh-TOOT.

765. ——— engravings.
——— in-NA'SH.

766. I should like to see the park.
A-nah AH-wiz a-SHOOF el-ge-NAY-nah. (M.)
A-nah OW-zah a-SHOOF el-ge-NAY-nah. (F.)

767. We should like to see [the park].
EĦ-nah ow-ZEEN ni-SHOOF [el-ge-NAY-nah].

768. —— **the Cathedral.**
—— el-ka-tid-rah-LEE-ya.

769. —— **the Citadel.**
—— el-al-AH.

770. —— **the library.**
—— el-mak-TA-ba.*

771. —— **the palace.**
—— el-AHS-re (OR is-sah-RAH-yah).

772. —— **the zoo.**
—— ge-NAY-net el-ḥa-ya-wa-NAT.

773. When does the museum [open] close?
EM-tah el-MAT-ḥuff [YIF-taḥ] YE'-fill?

774. Is this the way to [the entrance] the exit?
HEE-yah dee SIK-ket [id-doh-KHOOL] el-khoh-ROOG?

775. What is the price of admission?
bee-KAM id-doh-KHOOL?

776. If we have time, we shall visit the Fine Arts Gallery.
low may-AH-nah wah't ḥun-ROOḤ MAT-ḥuff el-foh-NOON el-ga-MEE-la.

A TRIP UP THE NILE

777. Where is the riverboat dock?
fayn mow-AF el-oh-toh-BEES in-NAH-ree?

* The term *mak TA ba* also means "stationer" and "bookshop."

778. How many [kilometers] is this trip?
ir-REH̱-la dee kam [KEE-loh]?

779. —— days?
—— yohm?

780. —— hours?
—— SA-a'?

781. How much does it cost (to go) to ——?
bee-KAM ir-REH̱-la lee ——?

782. Which is the nearest stop to [the Fayum (the largest Egyptian oasis)]?
ay AH'-rub BA-lud lee [el-fī-YOOM]?

783. —— Tel-el-Amarna (site of Akhenaten's temple)?
—— tull el-a-MAR-nah?

784. —— the [Luxor] Karnak Temple?
—— MAH-bud [el-LO'-sohr] el-KAR-nak?

785. —— the Valley of the Kings?
—— WAH-dee el-moh-LOOK?

786. —— the Abu Simbel Temple?
—— MAH-bud A-boo SIM-bel?

787. —— the Aga Khan's tomb?
—— mah'-BAH-ret ařa-KHAN?

788. —— Nubia?
—— in-NOO-ba?

THE CHURCH

789. A [Catholic] church.
ki-NEE-sa [ka-toh-lee-KEE-ya].

790. —— Protestant.
—— broh-tes-TANT.

791. —— Orthodox.
—— or-tho-zok-SEE-ya.

792. —— Coptic.
—— eb-TEE-ya.

793. Where is the [Virgin Mary] Church?
fayn ki-NEE-sit [el-AHD-ra MAR-yam]?

794. Is there an English-speaking [priest] here?
fee HE-nah [as-SEES] bee-yit-KAL-lim en-ge-LEE-zee?

795. At what time is the service?
is-sah-LAH EM-tah?

THE MOSQUE

796. The mosque.
ig-GA-meh.

797. The minaret.
el-MAD-na.

798. The pulpit.
el-man-BUR.

799. The imam.
el-ee-MAM.

800. The Friday prayer.
sah-LAHT el-GŪM-ah.

801. The caller to prayer.
el-mo-AZ-zin.

802. The call to prayer.*
el-a-DAN.

> **803. ahl-LAH-hoo AHK-bahr.**
> God is great.

> **804. ash-HA-doo AL-la ee-LA-ha IL-la ahl-LAH.**
> I witness that there is but one God.

> **805. ash-HA-doo AN-nah moh-ham-MA-dan rah-SOO-loo ahl-LAH.**
> I witness that Mohammed is His prophet.

> **806. hi AH-lah ahs-sah-LAH.**
> Come to prayer.

* It is always inspiring for peoples alien to Islam to hear the call to prayer in an Islamic country. The caller usually climbs to the highest levels of the minaret and from its balcony he calls Muslims to come to prayer. He also walks around so that his call can be heard from all directions. All the phrases, excepting the last, are repeated once. Spectators are welcomed to enter any mosque except during prayers. All people entering a mosque must take off their shoes as a sign of respect for the "House of God."

807. h̄i AH-lah al-fah-LAH̄.
Come to success.

808. ahl-LAH-hoo AHK-bahr.
God is great.

809. la ee-LAH-ha IL-la ahl-LAH.
There is no God but Him.

AMUSEMENTS

810. I should like to go to [a concert].
A-nah AH-wiz ah-ROOH̄ [kon-SHAYR-toh]. (M.)
A-nah OW-zah ah-ROOH̄ [kon-SHAYR-toh]. (F.)

811. We should like to go to [a concert].
EH̄-nah ow-ZEEN ni-ROOH̄ [kon-SHAYR-toh].

812. ——— the ballet.
——— el-ba-LAY.

813. ——— the theater.
——— el-MAHS-rah̄.

814. ——— the opera.
——— el-OB-rah.

815. ——— the movies.
——— is-SI-ne-mah.

816. ——— the folk dances.
——— ir-RA'-зc ish-SHAH-bee.

817. —— **the puppets.**
—— el-ah-rah-GOHZ.

818. —— **the marionettes.**
—— MAHS-raⁿ el-ah-RĪ-yis.

819. —— **the nightclub.**
—— ka-ba-RAY.

820. —— **the gambling casino.**
—— KA-zee-noh el-oh-MAHR.

821. —— **the belly dancers.**
—— ir-RA'-se el-BA-la-dee.

822. —— **the box office.**
—— shib-BAK it-ta-ZA-ker.

823. **Is there a matinee performance today?**
fee ḦUF-lah "matinee" in-nay-HAHR-dah?

824. **Have you any seats for tonight?**
fee ka-RA-see lil-lay-LA-dee?

825. **How much is [an orchestra seat]?**
bee-KAM [KŪR-see is-SAH-lah]?

826. —— **a balcony seat?**
—— KŪR-see ba-la-KOHN?

827. —— **a loge?**
—— lohg?

828. **May I have a program?**
AH'-dahr AH-khŭd ber-NA-mig?

829. Are there opera glasses for rent?
fee nud-dah-RAHT moh-uz-ZAH-mah lil-ee-GAHR?

830. Not too far from the stage.
mish bay-EED min el-MAHS-raḥ.

831. When does the program start?
EM-tah el-ber-NA-mig yib-TI-dee?

832. How long is the intermission?
el-is-te-RAH-ḥa ad-dee-AY?

833. What is the minimum charge?
bee-KAM AHR-khas tahz-KAH-rah?

834. May I have this dance?
tis-ma-ḤEE-lee bir-RAH'-sah dee?

835. Will you play a [fox trot]?
TE'-dahr TEL-ahb ["fox trot"]?

836. ——— mambo?
——— "mambo?"

837. ——— rumba?
——— "rumba?"

838. ——— samba?
——— "samba?"

839. ——— tango?
——— "tango?"

840. ——— waltz?
——— vahls?

841. ——— folk dance?
——— BA-la-dee?

SPORTS

842. We want to play [soccer].
EH-nah ow-ZEEN nel-AHB [KOH-rah].

843. ——— basketball.
——— BUS-kit.

844. ——— volleyball.
——— "volley."

845. ——— tennis.
——— "tennis."

846. ——— ping pong.
——— "ping pong."

847. ——— golf.
——— gūlf.

848. Let's go swimming.
YUL-lah ni-ROOH ni-OOM.

849. Let's go to [the swimming pool].
YUL-lah ni-ROOH [HUM-mam is-see-BA-ha].

850. ——— the soccer game.
——— "match" el-KOH-rah.

851. ——— the horse races.
——— SA-ba' el-KHAYL.

852. Let's go skeet shooting.
YUL-lah ni-ROOH it-TEE-roo.

853. I need [fishing tackle].
A-nah AH-wiz [sin-NAH-rah]. (M.)

854. **We need [fishing tackle (for more than one person)].**
EH-nah ow-ZEEN [sa-na-NEER].

855. ——— **a tennis racket.**
——— MUD-rub "tennis."

856. ——— **tennis rackets.**
——— mah-DAH-rib "tennis."

857. **Can we go [fishing]?**
NE'-dahr ni-ROOH [nis-TAHD]?

858. ——— **horseback riding?**
——— NIR-kub khayl?

859. ——— **roller skating?**
——— "skating?"

BANK AND MONEY

860. **Where is the nearest bank here?**
fayn AH'-rub bank HE-nah?

861. **At which window can I cash this check?**
AHS-rif ish-SHEEK da fayn?

862. **What is the exchange rate on the dollar?**
id-doh-LAHR bee-KAM?

863. **I have [a bank draft].**
may-I-yah [sheek mahs-RAH-fee].

864. ——— **a letter of credit.**
——— ga-WAB ay-tee-MAD.

865. ——— traveler's checks.
——— shee-KAT SA-far.

866. I would like to exchange twenty dollars for ———.
A-nah AH-wiz ah-H̄OW-will īsh-REEN doh-LAHR ———. (M.)
A-nah OW-zah ah-H̄OW-will īsh-REEN doh-LAHR ———. (F.)

867. Please change this for [large bills].
min-FAHD-luk R̄Ī-yahr dohl lee (WA-ra' ki-BEER). (TO M.)
min-FAHD-lik r̄ī-YAH-ree dohl lee (WA-ra' ki-BEER). (TO F.)

868. ——— small bills.
——— WA-ra' so-R̄Ī-yahr.

869. ——— small change.
——— FAK-kah so-r̄ī-YAH-rah.

870. Egyptian currency.
OHM-la mahs-REE-yah.

871. Pounds. (= about $2.30 U.S.)
ge-nay-HAT.

872. Piasters. (= about $.02 U.S.)
oh-ROOSH.

873. Millièmes. (= about $.002 U.S.)
ma-la-LEEM.

SHOPPING

874. I need some things.
A-nah AH-wiz SHWĬ-yit ĥa-GAT. (M.)
A-nah OW-zah SHWĬ-yit ĥa-GAT. (F.)

875. We need some things.
EĤ-nah ow-ZEEN SHWĬ-yit ĥa-GAT.

876. Can we shop for them?
NE'-dahr ni-ROOĤ nish-te-REE-ha?

877. Does anyone here speak English?
fee hahd HE-nah bee-yit-KAL-lim en-ge-LEE-zee?

878. I am just looking around.
A-nah but-FAHR-rug bass.

879. How much is it?
bee-KAM?

880. ——— per piece?
——— el-ĤIT-ta?

881. ——— per meter?
——— el-MIT-re?

882. ——— per pound?
——— ir-RUT-le?

883. ——— per kilo?
——— el-KEE-loh?

884. ——— per package?
——— el-LUF-fah?

885. ——— **per bunch?**
——— el-ḤIZ-ma?

886. ——— **all together?**
——— KŪL-loo AH-lah BAH-doh?

887. **It is [too expensive].**
da [ṚA-lee A-wee].

888. ——— **cheap.**
——— re-KHEES.

889. ——— **reasonable.**
——— mah-OOL.

890. **Is that your lowest price?**
da A-khir TA-man?

891. **Can I get a discount?**
AH'-dahr AH-khud takh-FEED?

892. **I [do not] like that.**
da [mish] ah-GIB-nee.

893. **Have you something [better]?**
fee AN-dak ḤA-ga [AḤ-san]? (TO M.)
fee AN-dik ḤA-ga [AḤ-san]? (TO F.)

894. ——— **cheaper?**
——— AHR-khas?

895. ——— **cuter?**
——— AHL-tuff?

896. ——— **softer?**
——— AN-ahm?

897. ——— **stronger?**
——— AG-mad?

898. —— **lighter (in weight)?**
—— a-KHUFF?

899. —— **tighter?**
—— AD-ya'?

900. —— **looser?**
—— OW-sah?

901. —— **lighter (in color)?**
—— AF-taȟ?

902. —— **darker?**
—— AȒ-ma'?

903. Show me something [of medium size].
wahr-REE-nee ȞA-ga [ma-AS AH-dee].

904. —— **of large size.**
—— ma-AS ki-BEER.

905. —— **of small size.**
—— ma-AS soo-ȒI-yahr.

906. —— **in a different style.**
—— MOH-dah TAN-ya.

907. May I try it on?
AH'-dahr ah-gahr-RUB-ha?

908. Will it shrink?
dee bit-KISH?

909. Is this color-fast?
el-LOHN da bee-YIB-hat?

910. This is [not] my size.
dee [mish] ma-A-see.

911. Can I order it?
AH'-dahr aht-LOHB-hah?

912. How long will it take to make the alterations?
it-tahs-LEEH̱ YA-khūd ad-dee-AY?

913. I shall come back later.
H̱AHR-gah ka-MAN SHWĬ-yah.

914. Will you please wrap this?
TE'-dahr tee-LIF dee min-FAHD-luk? (TO M.)
te'-DAH-ree tee-LIF-fee dee. min-FAHD-lik? (TO F.)

915. Where do I pay?
AD-fah fayn?

916. Can you send it to my hotel?
TE'-dahr teb-AHT-ha lil-loh-KAHN-dah? (TO M.)
te'-DAH-ree teb-ah-TEE-ha lil-loh-KAHN-dah? (TO F.)

917. Please pack this carefully for export.
min-FAHD-luk lif-FAH-ha KWĬ-yis AH̱-san ẖash-H̱IN-ha. (TO M.)
min-FAHD-lik lif-FEE-ha KWĬ-yis AH̱-san ẖash-H̱IN-ha. (TO F.)

918. Please give me [a bill].
min-FAHD-luk id-DEE-nee [a-SEE-ma]. (TO M.)
min-FAHD-lik id-DEE-nee [a-SEE-ma]. (TO F.)

919. ——— a receipt.
——— WAHS-le.

920. **I shall pay upon delivery.**
ḤUD-fah ahnd lis-tee-LAM.

921. **Is there an additional charge [for delivery]?**
fee OHG-rah zee-YA-da [lit-tow-SEEL]?

MEASUREMENTS

922. **Please take my measurements.**
min-FAHD-luk khūd ma-A-see. (TO M.)
min-FAHD-lik KHŪ-dee ma-A-see. (TO F.)

923. **What is [the size]?**
[el-ma-AS] ad-dee-AY?

924. ——— **the length?**
——— it-TOOL?

925. ——— **the width?**
——— el-AHRD?

926. ——— **the weight?**
——— it-TO'-le?

927. ——— **the volume?**
——— el-ḤAG-me?

928. **How long is this?**
TOL-hah ad-dee-AY dee?

929. Small.   **Smaller.**
soo-ṚĪ-yahr;   AHS-ṛahr.
soo-ṛī-YAH-rah.*

930. Large.   **Larger.**
ki-BEER;   AHK-bahr.
ki-BEE-ra.

931. High.   **Higher.**
AH-lee;   AH-lah.
AHL-yah.

932. Low.   **Lower.**
WAH-tee;   OW-tah.
WAHT-yah.

933. Long.   **Longer.**
tah-WEEL;   AHT-wahl.
tah-WEE-la.

934. Short.   **Shorter.**
oh-SĪ-yahr;   AH'-sahr.
oh-sī-YAH-rah.

935. Thin.   **Thinner.**
roo-FĪ-yah;   AHR-fah.
roo-fī-YAH-ah.

936. Thick.   **Thicker.**
te-KHEEN;   AT-khan.
te-KHEE-na.

937. Narrow.   **Narrower.**
DĪ-yi';   AD-ya'.
dī-YI-a.

* In sentences 929–940, the first form of the adjective given is masculine, the second feminine. There is no gender change in the comparative form.

938. **Wide.** **Wider.**
WAS-ya; OW-sah.
WAS-ah.

939. **Old.** **Older.**
a-DEEM; A'-dam.
a-DEE-ma.

940. **New.** **Newer.**
gi-DEED; AG-dad.
gi-DEE-da.

COLORS

941. **I want a [darker] lighter shade.**
A-nah AH-wiz lohn [AȒ-ma'] AF-taẖ. (M.)
A-nah OW-zah lohn [AȒ-ma'] AF-taẖ. (F.)

942. **Black.**
IS-wid; SOH-da.*

943. **Blue.**
AZ-ra'; ZAR-a.

944. **Brown.**
BON-nee.

945. **Cream.**
kraym.

946. **Grey.**
roh-SAH-see.

---

* In sentences 942, 943, 947, 951, 952 and 953, the first
form of the adjective given is masculine, the second feminine.
For the other colors given here there is no gender change.

947. Green.
AHKH-dahr; KHAHD-rah.

948. Orange.
bohr-too-A-nee.

949. Pink.
BAM-bee (OR BAM-bah).

950. Purple.
ba-naf-SIG-gee.

951. Red.
AH̱-mahr; H̱AHM-rah.

952. White.
AHB-yahd; BAY-dah.

953. Yellow.
AHS-fahr; SAHF-rah.

STORES

954. Is there [a supermarket] here?
fee HE-nah [gam-EE-ya]?

955. —— a bakery?
—— FOR-ne?

956. —— a bookshop?
—— mak-TA-ba?

957. —— a butcher?
—— gahz-ZAHR?

958. —— a candy shop?
—— mah-H̱AHL ḥa-la-wee-YAT?

959. —— **a cigar store?**
—— da-KHAKH-nee?

960. —— **a clothing store?**
—— mah-H̄AHL ho-DOOM?

961. —— **a dressmaker?**
—— TAR-zee h̄ah-REE-mee?

962. —— **a drug store** (OR **pharmacy**)?
—— ag-za-KHA-na?

963. —— **a florist?**
—— mah-H̄AHL zo-HOOR?

964. —— **a fruit store?**
—— ʃa-ka-HΛ-nee?

965. —— **a grocery store?**
—— ba'-AL?

966. —— **a hardware store?**
—— mah-H̄AHL hee-DA-da?

967. —— **a hat shop?**
—— mah-H̄AHL bah-rah-NEET?

968. —— **a jewelry store?**
—— ga-wa-HIR-gee (OR SA-yir̃)?

969. —— **a market?**
—— soo'?

970. —— **a music store?**
—— mah-H̄AHL es-to-wah-NAHT?

971. —— **a shoemaker?**
—— gaz-MA-gee?

972. ——— **a shoe store?**
——— mah-H̄AHL GI-zum?

973. ——— **a spice store?**
——— aht-TAHR?

974. ——— **a tailor?**
——— TAR-zee ri-GA-lee?

975. ——— **a toy shop?**
——— mah-H̄AHL lay-UB aht-FAHL?

976. ——— **a vegetable store?**
——— khūd-rah-WAH-tee?

977. ——— **a watchmaker?**
——— sa-AH-tee?

CLOTHING STORE

978. I want to buy ———.
A-nah AH-wiz ash-TE-ree ———. (M.)
A-nah OW-zah ash-TE-ree ———. (F.)

979. We would like to buy ———.
EH̄-nah ow-ZEEN nish-TE-ree ———.

980. ——— **a bathing cap.**
——— tah-EE-yit ohm.

981. ——— **a bathing suit.**
——— ma-YOH.

982. ——— **a blouse.**
——— BLOO-za.

983. ———— **a brassiere.**
———— son-tee-YAN.

984. ———— **a coat.**
———— BAHL-toh.

985. ———— **a collar.**
———— YA-ah.

986. ———— **some diapers.**
———— LI-fuff.

987. ———— **a dress.**
———— fos-TAN.

988. ———— **some children's dresses.**
———— ma-LA-bis aht-FAHL.

989. ———— **a pair of gloves.**
———— go-WAHN-tee.

990. ———— **a handbag.**
———— SHAHN-tah hah-REE-mee.

991. ———— **a dozen handkerchiefs.**
———— DAS-tit ma-na-DEEL.

992. ———— **a hat.**
———— bor-NAY-tah.

993. ———— **a jacket.**
———— ja-KIT-ta.

994. ———— **a necktie.**
———— kah-rah-VAHT-tah.

995. ———— **a nightgown.**
———— ah-MEES nohm.

996. ——— **a pair of pajamas.**
——— bee-JA-ma.

997. ——— **panties.**
——— kee-loht-TĀT.

998. ——— **a raincoat.**
——— BAHL-toh MAH-tahr.

999. ——— **a lady's scarf.**
——— shal.

1000. ——— **a man's scarf.**
——— tal-FEE-ah.

1001. ——— **a shirt.**
——— ah-MEES.

1002. ——— **a pair of shoes.**
——— gohz GAZ-ma.

1003. ——— **a shoelace.**
——— roh-BAHT GAZ-ma.

1004. ——— **sport shorts (for men).**
——— bun-tah-LOHN short.

1005. ——— **a skirt.**
——— jee-BOHN.

1006. ——— **a slip.**
——— ah-MEES taĥ-TA-nee.

1007. ——— **a pair of leather slippers.**
——— SHIB-shib.

1008. ——— **a pair of wooden slippers.**
——— ob-AB.

1009. ——— a man's suit.
——— BAD-la.

1010. ——— a pair of suspenders.
——— ham-ma-LAT.

1011. ——— a sweater.
——— "sweater" (OR BUL-loh-ver).

1012. ——— a pair of trousers.
——— bun-tah-LOHN.

1013. ——— men's underwear.
——— řee-yah-RAHT taĥ-ta-NEE-ya.

1014. ——— an undershirt.
——— ʃa-NIL-la.

1015. ——— a pair of undershorts.
——— li-BAS (OR kal-SOON).

DRY GOODS STORE

1016. Handkerchief.
man-DEEL.

1017. Pins.
da-ba-BEES.

1018. Common pin.
dub-BOOS.

1019. Hair pin.
dub-BOOS shahr.

1020. Safety pin.
dub-BOOS MASH-bak.

1021. Buttons.
zah-RAH-yer.

1022. Needle.
IB-ra.

1023. Brush.
FÜR-sha.

1024. Hairbrush.
FÜR-shit shahr.

1025. Shaving brush.
FÜR-shit ḥi-LA-ah.

1026. Toothbrush.
FÜR-shit is-NAN.

1027. Clothes brush.
FÜR-shit ho-DOOM.

1028. Lipstick.
AḤ-mahr sha-FA-yif (or "rouge").

1029. Nail polish.
ma-ni-KEER.

1030. Nail polish remover.
a-si-TOHN.

1031. Rouge.
BOD-ret wish.

1032. Shampoo.
"shampoo."

DRUG STORE OR PHARMACY

1033. Is there a [pharmacy] here?
fee HE-nah [ag-za-KHA-na]?

1034. Can you fill this prescription [immediately]?
TE'-dahr te-ḤUD-dahr da [AH-lah tool]?

1035. Do you have [adhesive tape]?
AN-dak [shi-REET laz']?

1036. —— alcohol?
—— see-BER-too AHB-yahd?

1037. —— "Alka-Seltzer?"
—— malḥ fow-WAHR?

1038. —— antiseptic?
—— moh-TAH-her?

1039. —— aspirin?
—— is-bi-REEN?

1040. —— bandage (OR gauze)?
—— shash?

1041. —— bicarbonate of soda?
—— kahr-boo-NAH-toh [OR bee-kahr-boh-NAHT is-SOH-dah]?

1042. —— boric acid?
—— ḤAH-mid boh-RAYK?

1043. —— a comb?
—— misht?

1044. ——— **a deodorant?**
——— moo-ZEEL ler-REE-ħa?

1045. ——— **a depilatory?**
——— moo-ZEEL lish-SHAHR?

1046. ——— **eyewash?**
——— ħa-SEEL oh-YOON?

1047. ——— **face cream?**
——— kraym lil-WISH?

1048. ——— **facial tissues?**
——— ma-na-DEEL WA-ra' (OR "Klee-nex")?

1049. ——— **hand lotion?**
——— kraym lil-ee-DAYN?

1050. ——— **hair cream?**
——— kraym lish-SHAHR?

1051. ——— **shaving cream?**
——— kraym ħay-LA-ah?

1052. ——— **skin cream?**
——— kraym lil-GILD?

1053. ——— **a hot water bottle?**
——— ER-bit MĪ-yah SOKH-nah?

1054. ——— **insect repellent?**
——— moh-BEED lil-ħah-shah-RAHT?

1055. ——— **iodine?**
——— SAB-ħit yood?

1056. ——— **a laxative?**
——— MOHS-hill?

1057. ——— **a medicine dropper?**
——— ut-TAH-rah?

1058. ——— **mouthwash?**
——— fah-SEEL lil-BO'?

1059. ——— **powder?**
——— BOD-rah?

1060. ——— **talcum powder?**
——— BOD-ret talk?

1061. ——— **a razor?**
——— moos?

1062. ——— **a package of razor blades?**
——— EL-bet im-WAS?

1063. ——— **a sedative?**
——— moo-NOW-wim?

1064. ——— **soap?**
——— sah-BOON?

1065. ——— **a pair of sunglasses?**
——— nud-DAH-rit shams?

1066. ——— **suntan oil?**
——— zayt SAB-rit shams?

1067. ——— **a thermometer?**
——— ter-moh-MIT-re?

1068. ——— **a tube of toothpaste?**
——— um-BOO-bit mah-GOON is NAN?

1069. ——— **a can of toothpowder (OR denture powder)?**
——— EL-bet BOD-ret is-NAN?

1070. —— **cotton wool?**
—— LUF-fit OT-ne?

CIGAR STORE

1071. Is the cigar store open?
HOO-wah id-da-KHAKH-nee FA-teħ?

1072. I want [a pack of American cigarettes].
A-nah AH-wiz [EL-bet sa-GA-yer am-ree-KA-nee]. (M.)
A-nah OW-zah [EL-bet sa-GA-yer am-ree-KA-nee]. (F.)

1073. —— **a pack of cigars.**
—— EL-bet "cigar."

1074. —— **a cigar.**
—— "cigar."

1075. —— **matches.**
—— kab-REET.

1076. —— **a pipe.**
—— BEE-ba.

1077. —— **pipe tobacco.**
—— doh-KHAHN lil-BEE-ba.

1078. —— **a lighter.**
—— wahl-LA-ah.

1079. —— **lighter fluid.**
—— ban-ZEEN wahl-LA-ah.

1080. ———— **flint.**
———— H̱AH-gahr wahl-LA-ah.

BOOKSHOP AND STATIONER

1081. Is there [a bookshop] around here?
fee [mak-TA-ba] HE-nah?

1082. ———— **a newsdealer?**
————bī-YAH gah-RAH-yed?

1083. I want to buy [a book].
A-nah AH-wiz ash-TE-ree [ki-TAB]. (M.)
A-nah OW-zah ash-TE-ree [ki-TAB]. (F.)

1084. ———— **a deck of playing cards.**
———— kot-SHAY-nah.

1085. ———— **an Arabic-English dictionary.**
———— qah-MOOS AH-rah-bee en-ge LEE-zee.

1086. ———— **an English-Arabic dictionary.**
———— qah-MOOS en-ge-LEE-zee AH-rah-bee.

1087. ———— **a dozen envelopes.**
———— DUS-tit oz-ROFF ga-wa-BAT.

1088. ———— **an eraser.**
———— as-TEE-ka.

1089. ———— **folders.**
———— doh-say-HAT.

1090. ——— **ink.**
——— H̄IB-re.

1091. ——— **a map.**
——— khah-REE-tah.

1092. ——— **some magazines.**
——— me-gal-LAT.

1093. ——— **a newspaper.**
——— ga-REE-da.

1094. ——— **a notebook.**
——— kahr-RAHS.

1095. ——— **a lecture notebook.**
——— kash-KOOL.

1096. ——— **a small notebook.**
——— NOH-ta.

1097. ——— **carbon paper.**
——— WA-ra' kur-BOHN.

1098. ——— **onionskin paper.**
——— WA-ra' khah-FEEF.

1099. ——— **writing paper.**
——— WA-ra' ga-wa-BAT.

1100. ——— **fountain pen.**
——— A-lam H̄IB-re.

1101. ——— **ballpoint pen.**
——— A-lam H̄IB-re gaf.

1102. ——— **a pencil.**
——— A-lam roo-SAHS.

1103. —— **postcards.**
—— kroot BOHS-tah.

1104. —— **a roll of string.**
—— LUF-fit doh-BAH-rah.

1105. —— **tape.**
—— shi-REET.

1106. —— **masking tape.**
—— shi-REET laz'.

1107. —— **Scotch tape.**
—— "cello-tape."

1108. —— **a typewriter.**
—— A-la KAT-ba.

1109. —— **typewriter ribbon.**
—— shi-REET A-la KAT-ba.

BARBER SHOP

1110. Where is there a good [barber shop]?
fee HE-nah [ĥul-LA'] KWĬ-yis?

1111. I would like to have my hair cut.
A-nah AH-wiz AĤ-la'.

1112. Don't cut too much.
mut-OS-sish ke-TEER.

1113. Don't cut any off the top, please.
KHUF-fif el-A-fa wil ga-WA-nib bass,
min-FAHD-luk.

1114. I part my hair [on the side].
A-nah BAF-ri' SHAH-ree [AH-lah el-GANB].

1115. ———— on the other side.
———— AH-lah el-GANB it-TA-nee.

1116. ———— in the middle.
———— fin-NOS.

1117. No hair tonic, please.
· ba-LASH faz-LEEN min-FAHD-luk.

1118. A shave (LIT.: chin).
DA'-ne.

BEAUTY PARLOR

1119. I want to [cut] [wash] my hair.
A-nah OW-zah [ah-OS] [AR̃-sil] SHAH-ree.

1120. Not too short.
mish oh-SĪ-yahr AH-wee.

1121. A hair set.
"coiffure."

1122. Hair tint.
SAB-r̃it shahr.

1123. Wave.
MOH-gah.

1124. A permanent wave.
MUK-wah.

1125. A manicure.
ma-nee-KEER.

1126. A massage.
"massage."

1127. A shampoo.
"shampoo."

1128. Can I make an appointment for ———?
AH'-dahr a-KHŬD may-AD AH-lah shan
———?

CAMERA SHOP AND PHOTOS

1129. I want a roll of film for this camera.
A-nah AH-wiz film lil-"camera" dee. (M.)
A-nah OW-zah film lil-"camera" dee. (F.)

1130. Do you have [color film]?
AN-dak [film mi-LOW-win]?

1131. ——— black-and-white film?
——— film AHB-yahd WIS-wid?

1132. ——— movie film?
——— film SI-ne-mah?

1133. ——— flashbulbs?
——— LOH-mud flash?

1134. ——— a tripod?
——— ḤAH-mill lil-"camera?"

1135. What is the charge [for developing a roll]?
bee-KAM [taḥ-MEED el-FILM]?

1136. —— **for enlarging?**
—— it-tak-BEER?

1137. —— **for one print?**
—— is-SOO-rah?

1138. Please have this ready soon.
min-FAHD-luk   khahl-LAHS-hah   bee-SŪR-ah.

1139. May I take a shot of you?
AH'-dahr a-KHŪD-luk SOO-rah? (TO M.)
AH'-dahr a-KHŪD-lik SOO-rah? (TO F.)
AH'-dahr a-khūd-LOH-kūm SOO-rah?
(TO GR.)

1140. Would you take a photo for me, please?
MOHM-kin ta-KHŪD-lee SOO-rah min-FAHD-luk? (TO M.)
MOHM-kin takh-DEE-lee SOO-rah min-FAHD-lik? (TO F.)

1141. Would you take a photo for us, please?
MOHM-kin ta-khūd-LI-na SOO-rah min-FAHD-luk? (TO M.)
MOHM-kin takh-DIL-na SOO-rah min-FAHD-lik? (TO F.)

LAUNDRY AND DRY CLEANING

1142. Where can I take my laundry to be washed?
AH'-dahr AŘ-sill ho-DOO-mee fayn?

1143. Is there a dry-cleaning service around here?

fee HE-nah tan-toor-LAY oh-RĬ-yib?

1144. I would like to wash these.

A-nah AH-wiz AR̄-sill dohl. (M.)

A-nah OW-zah AR̄-sill dohl. (F.)

1145. This is to be washed in [hot water].

dee lil-r̄a-SEEL fee [MĬ-yah SOKH-nah].

1146. —— warm water.

—— MĬ-yah DUF-ya.

1147. —— lukewarm water.

—— MĬ-yah FAT-ra.

1148. —— cold water.

—— MĬ-yah BAR-da.

1149. Do not wash this in hot water.

ma-tir̄-SIL-she dee fee MĬ-yah SOKH-nah.

1150. Can you remove this stain?

TE'-dahr ti-TAHL-lah el-BO'-ah dee?
(TO M.)

te'-DAH-ree tc-tahl-LAH-ee el-BO'-ah dee?
(TO F.)

1151. Starch the collar.

NASH-shee el-YA-ah.

1152. Do not use starch.

ba-LASH NI-sha.

1153. I want this suit cleaned and pressed.

A-nah AH-wiz el-BAD-la dee tet-RĬ-sill wi
tet-KĬ-wee. (M.)

1154. The pocket is torn.
el-GAYB makh-ROO'.

1155. Can you sew on this button?
TE'-dahr te-RAK-kib iz-zoo-RAHR da?
(TO M.)

te'-DAH-ree te-rak-KIB-ee iz-zoo-RAHR
da? (TO F.)

1156. Replace the old zipper with a new one.
RAK-kib SOS-ta gi-DEE-da. (TO M.)
rak-KIB-ee SOS-ta gi-DEE-da. (TO F.)

REPAIRS

1157. My watch is not working any more.
SA-tee WI'-fit.

1158. This clock [is fast] is slow.
is-SA-a' dee [bit-AD-dim] bit-AHKH-
khur.

1159. My glasses are broken.
in-nud-DAH-rah bi-TAH-tee mak-SOO-
rah.

1160. Where can I repair it?
AH'-dahr ah-sahl-LAH-hah fayn?

**1161. I would like to have my hearing aid
[adjusted] [repaired].**
A-nah AH-wiz [AHZ-bott] [ah-SAHL-
lah] is-sam-ma-AHT. (M.)
A-nah OW-zah [AHZ-bott] [ah-SAHL-
lah] is-sam-ma-AHT. (F.)

1162. Repair [the sole].
SAHL-laĥ in-NAHL.

1163. —— the heel.
—— el-KAHB.

1164. —— the uppers.
—— el-GILD.

1165. —— the strap.
—— el-ib-ZEEM.

HEALTH AND ILLNESS

1166. I wish to visit [a physician].
Λ-nah AH-wiz ah-ROOĤ lee [dok-TOHR
bah-TI-nee]. (M.)
A-nah OW-zah ah-ROOĤ lee [dok-TOHR
bah-TI-nee]. (F.)

1167. —— a doctor who speaks English.
—— dok-TOHR bee-yit-KAL-lim en-ge-
LEE-zee.

1168. —— a specialist.
—— ah-khis-SAH-ee.

1169. —— an orthopedist.
—— dok-TOHR ee-ZAHM.

1170. —— an oculist.
—— tah-BEEB ʋ-YOON.

1171. —— ear, nose and throat specia——.
—— ah-khis-SAH-ee AN-ſe wi O-zun wi
ĥahn-GAH-rah.

1172. ——— a dentist.
——— tah-BEEB is-NAN.

1173. **Is the doctor [at home] in his office?**
id-dok-TOHR [fill bayt] fill ay-YA-da?

1174. **I have something in my eye.**
fee ḤA-ga fee AY-nee.

1175. **I have a pain in my back.**
DAH-ree bee-yoh-GAH-nee.

1176. **I do not sleep well.**
mah-bah-NAM-she KWĬ-yis.

1177. **Can you give me something to relieve the pain?**
TE'-dahr tid-DEE-nee moo-SAK-kin?

1178. **An allergy.**
ḥa-sa-SEE-ya.

1179. **An anesthetic.**
moo-KHAD-dir.

1180. **An appendicitis attack.**
el-tee-HAB fill mūs-RAHN.

1181. **An insect bite.**
AHR-sit ḤAH-shah-rah.

1182. **An abscess.**
DIM-mill.

1183. **A blister.**
fas-FOO-sa.

1184. A boil.
khŭr-RAHG.

1185. A burn.
ħar'.

1186. A cold.
bard.

1187. Constipation.
im-SAK.

1188. A cough.
KOĦ-ħa.

1189. A cramp.
mah-ŘUS.

1190. Diarrhoea.
is-HAL.

1191. Dysentery.
di-son-TΛR-ya.

1192. An earache.
WAH-gah fill wi-DAN.

1193. A fever.
ĦOHM-ma.

1194. Hay fever.
ZAK-ma SAY-fee.

1195. Headache.
soo-DAH'.

1196. Indigestion.
OS-re HUD-me.

1197. Measles.
ḤAHS-bah.

1198. German measles.
ḤAHS-bah al-MA-nee.

1199. Nausea.
QAY-a'.

1200. Pneumonia.
el-tee-HAB REE-a-wee.

1201. A sore throat.
el-tee-HAB el-ḤAL'.

1202. A sunburn.
el-tee-HAB el-GILD.

1203. Tonsilitis.
LEE-waz.

1204. Toothache.
WAH-gah is-NAN.

1205. What shall I do?
AH-mill ay?

1206. Do I have to go to [a hospital]?
LA-zim ah-ROOḤ [mūs-TASH-fa]?

1207. Is it contagious?
HOO-wah MOH-dee?

1208. I feel better.
A-nah AḤ-san SHWĬ-yah.

1209. There is no improvement.
mah-FEESH ta-ḤAHS-sūn.

1210. Can I travel Monday?
AH'-dahr a-SA-fir yohm lit-NAYN?

1211. When will you come again?
ħah-TEE-gee TA-nee EM-tah?

1212. When should I take [the medicine]?
EM-tah AH-khŭd [id-DA-wa]?

1213. —— the injections?
—— el-ĦOH-ahn?

1214. —— the pills?
—— el-ħoh-BOOB?

1215. Every hour.
kŭll SA-a'.

1216. [Before] [after] meals.
[AB-le] [bahd] el-AK-le.

1217. On going to bed.
AB-le in-NOHM.

1218. On getting up.
is-SOB-ħe.

1219. Twice a day.
mahr-ri-TAYN fill yohm.

1220. A drop.
NO'-tah.

1221. A teaspoonful
mah-LAH-a' soo-rī-YAH-rah.

1222. X-rays.
a-SHEE-ah.

DENTIST

1223. **Do you know a good [dentist]?**
EN-tah TAY-ruff (dok-TOHR is-NAN)
KWĬ-yis? (TO M.)
EN-tee tay-RUF-fee (dok-TOHR is-NAN)
KWĬ-yis? (TO F.)

1224. **I have lost a filling.**
ḤAHSH-we DIR-see wee-AH.

1225. **Can you fix [the filling]?**
TE'-dahr tee-SAHL-laḥ (el-ḤAHSH-we)?

1226. ———— **the bridge?**
———— el-KŪB-ree?

1227. ———— **this denture?**
———— it-TAH'-me da?

1228. **This front tooth hurts me.**
is-SIN-nah dee bee-toh-GAH-nee.

1229. **This [molar] hurts me.**
[id-DIR-se] da bee-yoh-GAH-nee.

1230. ———— **wisdom tooth.**
———— sin el-AH'-le.

1231. **I think I have [a broken tooth].**
iz-ZAH-her AN-dee [SIN-nah mak-SOO-rah].

1232. ———— **an abscess.**
———— DIM-mill.

1233. Please give me [gas (ether)].
min-FAHD-luk id-DEE-nee [ee-TAYR].

1234. —— a [local] anesthetic.
—— bing [mow-DI-ee].

ACCIDENTS

1235. There has been an accident.
fee ḤUD-sa.

1236. Please get [a doctor].
min-FAHD-luk   OT-lohb   [dok-TOHR].
(TO M.)
min-FAHD-lik ot-LOH-bee [dok-TOHR].
(TO F.)

1237. —— an ambulance.
—— el-is-AHF.

1238. —— a nurse.
—— moo-mah-REE-dah.

1239. —— a policeman.
—— as-KA-ree boh-LEES (OR SHOHR-
tee).

1240. He has fallen.
wee-AH.

1241. She has fainted.
OHṚ-ma a-LAY-ha.

1242. He has a cut.
et-OW-wahr.

1243. A fracture [in the arm] in the leg.
KAS-re [fill-EED] fir-RIG-le.

1244. A sprain.
MAL-khe.

1245. Bleeding.
na-ZEEF.

1246. Poisoning.
ta-SUM-mom.

1247. Swelling.
WAH-rum.

1248. I want to [rest] [sit down] a moment.
A-nah   AH-wiz   [ast-RĬ-yaḣ]   [A'-od]
    SHWĬ-yah. (M.)
A-nah   OW-zah   [ast-RĬ-yaḣ]   [A'-od]
    SHWĬ-yah. (F.)

1249. Please notify [my husand].
min-FAHD-luk ID-dee KHAH-bahr [lee
    GOH-zee]. (TO M.)
min-FAHD-lik ID-dee KHAH-bahr [lee
    GOH-zee]. (TO F.)

1250. ——— my wife.
——— lim-RAH-tee.

1251. ——— my friend.
——— lee SAḢ-bee.

PARTS OF THE BODY

1252. The appendix.
el-mūs-RAHN.

1253. The arm.
id-dee-RAH.

1254. The arteries.
el-oh-ROO'.

1255. The back.
id-DAH-re.

1256. The blood.
id-DUM.

1257. The bones.
el-AHD-me.

1258. The brain.
el-MOHKH.

1259. The breast.
el-bi-ZAZ.

1260. The cheek.
el-KHUD.

1261. The chest.
is-SID-re.

1262. The chin.
id-DA'-ne.

1263. The collarbone.
it-tohr-OH-wah.

1264. The ear.
el-WID-ne.

1265. The elbow.
el-KOO'.

1266. The eye.
el-AYN.

1267. The eyebrows.
el-ḥa-WA-gib.

1268. The eyelashes.
el-roo-MOOSH.

1269. The eyelid.
el-GIF-ne.

1270. The face.
el-WISH.

1271. The finger.
is-SAHB-yah.

1272. The fingernail.
DAH-fer SAHB-yah el-EED.

1273. The foot.
ir-RIG-le.

1274. The gall bladder.
el-ma-SA-na.

1275. The glands.
el-ṘOH-dud.

1276. The gums.
el-LIS-sa.

1277. The hair.
ish-SHAHR.

1278. The hand.
el-EED.

1279. The head.
ir-RAHS.

1280. The heart.
el-ALB.

1281. The heel.
el-KAHB.

1282. The hip.
el-WIR-ke.

1283. The intestines.
el-mah-sah-REEN.

1284. The jaw.
el-FAK.

1285. The joints.
el-mah-FAH-sill.

1286. The kidney.
el-KIL-ya.

1287. The knee.
ir-ROHK-bah.

1288. The leg.
ir-RIG-le.

1289. The lips.
ish-sha-FA-yif.

1290. The liver.
el-KIBD.

1291. The lungs.
ir-ree-a-TAYN.

1292. The mouth.
el-BO'.

1293. The muscles.
el-ah-dah-LAHT.

1294. The nail.
id-DAH-fer.

1295. The neck.
ir-RA-a-ba.

1296. The nerves.
el-ah-SAHB.

1297. The nose.
el-ma-na-KHEER.

1298. The ribs.
id-doh-LOO'.

1299. The shoulder.
el-KITF.

1300. The skin.
el-GILD.

1301. The skull.
el-gūm-GOH-ma.

1302. The spine.
sill-SI-lit id-DAH-re.

1303. The stomach.
el-MAH-ee-da.

1304. The teeth.
is-see-NAN.

1305. The toe.
SAHB-yah ir-RIG-le.

1306. The toenail.
DAH-fer SAHB-yah ir-RIG-le.

1307. The tongue.
el-lee-SAN.

1308. The tonsils.
el-LEE-wahz.

1309. The veins.
el-oh-ROO'.

1310. The wrist.
ir-RŪS-řc.

TIME

1311. What time is it?
is-SA-a' kam?

1312. Early.
BAD-ree.

1313. Late.
met-AHKII-khahr.

1314. Two A.M.
et-NAYN is-SOB-ḥc.

1315. Two P.M.
et-NAYN bahd id-DOH-rc.

1316. Half-past three.
ta-LA-ta wi noss.

1317. Quarter-past four.
ahr-BAH-ah wi rob'.

1318. Quarter to five.
KHAM-sa IL-la rob'.

1319. At ten minutes to six.
is-SA-a' SIT-ta IL-la AH-shah-rah.

1320. At twenty minutes past seven.
is-SA-a' SAB-ah wi tilt.

1321. In the morning.
is-SOB-ħe.

1322. In the afternoon.
bahd id-DOH-re.

1323. In the evening.
el-AHS-re.

1324. At noon.
id-DOH-re.

1325. The day.
in-nah-HAHR.

1326. The night.
el-LAYL.

1327. Midnight.
noss el-LAYL.

1328. Last night.
el-LAY-la IL-lee FA-tet.

1329. Yesterday.
em-BA-reĥ.

1330. Today.
in-nay-HAHR-dah.

1331. Tonight.
el-lay-LA-dee.

1332. Tomorrow.
BOK-rah.

1333. Last month.
ish-SHAH-re IL-lee fat.

1334. Last year.
is-SA-na IL-lee FA-tet.

1335. Next Sunday.
el-ĤUD IL-lee gī.

1336. Next week.
el-ohs-BOO' IL-lee gī.

1337. The day before yesterday.
OW-will em-BA-reĥ.

1338. The day after tomorrow.
bahd BOK-rah.

1339. Two weeks ago.
min ohs-boo-AYN FA-too.

WEATHER

1340. How is the weather today?
iz-ZĪ el-GOW in-nay-HAHR-dah?

1341. Cold.
bard.

1342. Fair.
AH-dee.

1343. Warm.
DA-fee.

1344. Very warm.
DA-fee GID-dan.

1345. Hot.
ħahr.

1346. Sunny.
MŪSH-miss.

1347. Beautiful.
ga-MEEL.

1348. It is raining.
id-DIN-ya bit-MUT-tahr (OR be-TISH-tee).

1349. I want to sit [in the shade].
A-nah AH-wiz A'-od [fid-DILL]. (M.)
A-nah OW-zah A'-od [fid-DILL]. (F.)

1350. —— in the sun.
—— fish-SHAMS.

1351. —— in a breeze.
—— fit-tah-RAH-wah.

DAYS OF THE WEEK

1352. Monday.
lit-NAYN.

1353. Tuesday.
it-ta-LAT.

1354. Wednesday.
LAHR-bah.

1355. Thursday.
el-kha-MEES.

1356. Friday.
ig-GOHM-ah.*

1357. Saturday.
is-SABT.

1358. Sunday.
el-ḤUD.

HOLIDAYS

1359. A public holiday.
yohm a-GA-za.

1360. Happy birthday (OR **Season's greetings**).
kūll SA-na WEN-ta TĪ-yib.

1361. Christmas.
eed el-mee-LAD.

* The Sabbath, which is the day of rest and of the midday collective prayer in all Islamic countries.

1362. Christian fasting month.
is-SOHM el-ki-BEER.

1363. Muslim fasting month.
rah-mah-DAHN.

1364. The feast.*
el-EED.

1365. Easter.†
eed el-ee-YA-ma.

1366. Good Friday.
ig-GOHM-ah el-ya-TEE-ma.

1367. The Christian year.
is-SA-na el-mee-la-DEE-ya.

1368. The Islamic year.
is-SA-na el-hig-REE-ya.

MONTHS AND SEASONS

1369. January.
ya-NA-yer.

---

* There are two main Muslim feasts. One concludes the fasting month of *rah-mah-DAHN* and is called *el-EED is-soo-RĪ-yahr* (or eed el-FIT-re), and the other (about two months later) is the sacrifice feast (commemorating Abraham's sacrifice of the ram in place of his son Isaac) known as *el-EED el-ki-BEER* (or eed el-AHD-ḥah).

†A local holiday that always falls on Easter Monday is called *sham in-ne-SEEM*.

1370. February.
fib-RĬ-yer.

1371. March.
MA-ris.

1372. April.
ab-REEL.

1373. May.
MA-yoo.

1374. June.
YO-ne-yah.

1375. July.
YO-le-yah.

1376. August.
ah-RŌS-tos.

1377. September.
"September."

1378. October.
"October."

1379. November.
"November."

1380. December.
"December."

1381. The spring.
ir-rah-BEE'.

1382. The summer.
is-SAYF.

1383. The autumn.
el-khah-REEF.

1384. The winter.
ish-SHI-ta.

USEFUL ARTICLES

1385. An ashtray.
tuf-FĪ-yit sa-GA-yer (OR mun-FAH-dah).

1386. A basket.
SA-bat.

1387. A bottle opener.
fut-TA-ħet a-ZĪ-yiz.

1388. A box.
san-DOO'.

1389. A bracelet.
ɼoh-WAY-sha.

1390. Brass.
ne-ĦAS AHS-fahr.

1391. A broom.
may-ASH-sha.

1392. A light bulb.
LAHM-bah.

1393. A camel.
GA-mal.

1394. A can opener.
fut-TA-ħet AY-lub.

1395. China.
sayr-VEES (OR SAY-nee).

1396. A clock.
SA-it ħayt.

1397. An alarm clock.
mi-NUB-bih.

1398. Cotton.
OT-ne.

1399. A silver compact.
EL-bet BOD-rah.

1400. Copper.
ne-ĦAS.

1401. Cork.
fill.

1402. A corkscrew.
fut-TA-ħet el-FIL-la.

1403. A cork stopper.
FIL-la.

1404. A metal stopper.
[ŘAH-tah ee-ZA-za] [OR si-DA-da].

1405. A cushion.
MAS-nad.

1406. A dog.
kalb.

1407. A doll.
ah-ROO-sah (also means a bride).

1408. A donkey.
ḥoh-MAHR.

1409. Earrings.
ḤA-la'.

1410. Embroidery.
taht-REEZ.

1411. A flashlight.
but-tah-REE-yah.

1412. Chewing gum.
lee-BAN.

1413. A hairnet.
sha-ba-KIT shahr.

1414. Hair pins (also bobby pins).
da-ba-BEES shahr.

1415. A handbag.
SHAHN-tah.

1416. A hassock.
MAS-nad rig-LAYN.

1417. A horse.
ḥoh-SAHN.

1418. Gold.
DA-hub.

1419. Jewelry.
ga-WA-hir.

1420. Lace.
dun-TIL-la.

1421. Leather.
gild.

1422. Linen.
kit-TAN.

1423. Dress material.
o-MASH.

1424. A mirror.
me-RA-ya.

1425. Porcelain.
SAY-ncc.

1426. Matches (OR **sulphur**).
kab-REET.

1427. A box of matches.
EL-bet kab-REET.

1428. A mosquito net.
na-moo-SEE-ya.

1429. Musical instruments.
a-LAT moo-see-QI-ya.

1430. Sheet music.
NOH-ta moo-see-QI-ya.

1431. A nail file.
us-SAH-fah.

1432. A necklace.
O'-de.

1433. A needle.
EB-ra.

1434. A pacifier.
buz-ZA-za.

1435. A pail.
GAR-dal.

1436. A penknife.
MUT-wah.

1437. Perfume.
REE-ħa.

1438. A plate.
TAH-bah'.

1439. Phonograph records.
es-too-wah-NAHT.

1440. A radio.
RAH-dee-yoh.

1441. A ring.
KHA-tim.

1442. A rug.
sig-GA-da.

1443. Sandals.
SUN-dull.

1444. A scarf.
shal.

1445. Scissors.
may-US.

1446. Silk.
ḥah-REER.

1447. Silver.
FAHD-dah.

1448. A precious stone.
ḤAH-gahr ka-REEM.

1449. A tablecloth.
MUF-rush.

1450. A thimble.
kohs-tee-BAN.

1451. Thread.
khayt.

1452. Toys.
lay-UB.

1453. A tray.
sah-NEE-ya.

1454. An umbrella (OR **parasol**).
sham-SEE-ya.

1455. A vase.
zoh-REE-ya.

1456. A whiskbroom.
FŪR-shit hoh-DOOM.

1457. A wrist watch.
SA-it eed.

1458. Wire.
silk.

1459. Wood.
KHA-shab.

1460. Wool.
soof.

NUMBERS: CARDINALS

ENGLISH	ARABIC	SOUND
1461. 0	٠	SIF-re
1	١	WAH-ħed
2	٢	et-NAYN
3	٣	ta-LA-ta
4	٤	ahr-BAH-ah
5	٥	KHAM-sa
6	٦	SIT-ta
7	٧	SAB-ah
8	٨	ta-MAN-ya
9	٩	TES-ah
10	١٠	AH-shah-rah
11	١١	ħe-DAH-sher
12	١٢	et-NAH-sher
13	١٣	tah-laht-TAH-sher
14	١٤	ahr-bah-TAH-sher
15	١٥	khah-mahs-TAH-sher
16	١٦	sit-TAH-sher
17	١٧	sah-bah-TAH-sher
18	١٨	tah-mahn-TAH-sher
19	١٩	tes-sah-TAH-sher
20	٢٠	ish-REEN

ENGLISH	ARABIC	SOUND
21	٢١	WAH-ħed wi īsh-REEN
22	٢٢	et-NAYN wi īsh-REEN
30	٣٠	ta-la-TEEN
31	٣١	WAH-ħed wi ta-la-TEEN
40	٤٠	ar-bay-EEN
50	٥٠	kham-SEEN
60	٦٠	sit-TEEN
70	٧٠	sab-EEN
80	٨٠	ta-ma-NEEN
90	٩٠	tes-EEN
100	١٠٠	MAY-ya
101	١٠١	MAY-ya wi WAH-ħed
110	١١٠	MAY-ya wi AH-shah-rah
1,000	١ر٠٠٠	alf
2,000	٢ر٠٠٠	al-FAYN
3,000	٣ر٠٠٠	ta-LAT ta-LAF
4,000	٤ر٠٠٠	AHR-bah ta-LAF
5,000	٥ر٠٠٠	KHA-mas ta-LAF
100,000	١٠٠ر٠٠٠	meet alf
1,000,000	١ر٠٠٠ر٠٠٠	mill-YOHN

NUMBERS: ORDINALS*

1462. The first.

el-OW-wahl, el-ΟΟ-la.

* In this section, the first Arabic form given is MASC., the
second FEM. When only one form appears, it is used with
both MASC. and FEM. nouns.

The second.
it-TA-nee, it-TAN-ya.
The third.
it-TA-lit, it-TAL-la.
The fourth.
ir-RAH-byah, ir-RAHB-ah.
The fifth.
el-KHA-mis, el-KHAM-sa.
The sixth.
is-SA-dis, is-SAD-sa.
The seventh.
is-SA-byah, is-SAB-ah.
The eighth.
it-TA-min, it-TAM-nah.
The ninth.
it-TA-syah, it-TAS-ah.
The tenth.
el-AH-sher, el-AHSH-rah.
The twentieth.
el-ish-REEN.
The thirtieth.
it-ta-la-TEEN.

APPENDIX A

IMPORTANT ARAB COUNTRIES AND CITIES

In the following list only cities of importance to tourism are included. The first city listed under each country is the capital. Population figures are taken from the *Encyclopedia Americana*, 1964 Annual. Excluded from these figures is the number of Arab refugees from Palestine (about one and one-half million), residing mainly in Egypt, Jordan, Lebanon and Syria. Portions of the Arab World that do not constitute countries, such as Aden, Muskut (Muscat), Oman, etc. are not included in this list.

Algeria (el-ga-ZA-yer). 917,535 sq. mi.; pop. 11,300,000, *ca.* 1962.

Algiers (el-ga-ZA-yer); pop. 884,000.
Oran (oh-RAHN); pop. 393,000.

Egypt [The United Arab Republic] (MAHS-re [el-gom-hoh-REE-ya el-ah-rah-BEE-ya el-mūt-TA-ḥi-da]). 386,000 sq. mi.; pop. 27,303,000, *ca.* 1963.

Cairo (el-qah-HI-rah OR MAHS-re); pop. 3,346,000.

Alexandria (is-ken-de-REE-ya); pop. 1,513,000.
Port Said (boor sa-EED); pop. 244,000.

Iraq (el-ay-RA'). 171,599 sq. mi.; pop. 6,687,000,
ca. 1962.

Baghdad (baĭ-DAD); pop. 830,000.
Mosul (el-MOO-sill); pop. 180,000.
Basra (el-BAHS-rah); pop. 165,000.
Kirkuk (kar-KOOK); pop. 150,000.

Jordan (el-OR-don). 37,300 sq. mi.; pop.
1,727,000, *ca.* 1962.

Amman (AM-man); pop. 245,000.
Bethlehem (bayt laĥm); pop. 68,000.
Jericho (el-kha-LEEL); pop. 66,000.
Jerusalem (el-OD-se); pop. 60,000.

Kuwait (el-koo-WAYT). 6,000 sq. mi.; pop.
325,000, *ca.* 1963.

Kuwait (el-koo-WAYT); pop. 200,000.

Lebanon (lib-NAN). 4,015 sq. mi.; pop. 1,720,000
ca. 1962.

Beirut (bĭ-ROOT); pop. 500,000.
Tripoli (tah-RUB-lūs); pop. 145,000.
Sidon (SĬ-dah); pop. 25,000.

Libya (LIB-ya). 679,358 sq. mi.; pop. 1,244,000,
ca. 1962.

Tripoli (tah-RUB-lūs el-ŘAHRB); pop. 196,000.
Benghazi (BA-nee ŘA-zee); pop. 78,000.

Morocco (el-MAR̆-rib OR mur-RA-kish). 171,305 sq. mi.; pop. 11,925,000, *ca.* 1961.

Rabat (ir-rah-BAHT); pop. 227,445.

Casablanca   (id-DAHR   el-BAY-dah);   pop. 965,277.

Marrakech (mur-RA-kish); pop. 243,134.

Tangier (TUN-gah); pop. 141,714.

Saudi Arabia (is-soo-oo-DEE-ya). 800,000 sq. mi.; pop. more than 3,000,000, *ca.* 1963.

Riyadh (ir-ree-YAHD); pop. 169,185.

Mecca (MUK-kah); pop. 158,908.

Jiddah (GUD-dah); pop. 147,859.

Medina (el-ma-DEE-nah); pop. 71,998.

Sudan   (is-soo-DAN).   967,000   sq.   mi.;   pop. 12,640,000, *ca.* 1963.

Khartoum (el-khar-TOOM); pop. 93,103.

Omdurman (ŭm dŭr-MAHN); pop. 113,551.

El Obeid (el-oh-BĬ-yid); pop. 56,970.

Syria (SŪR-ya). 72,000 sq. mi.; pop. 5,067,000, *ca.* 1962.

Damascus   (dee-MASH'   OR   ish-SHAM);   pop. 507,503.

Aleppo (H̆A-lub); pop. 496,083.

Homs (H̆IM-se); pop. 164,762.

Latakia (el-la-zi-EE-ya); pop. 68,498.

Tunisia (TOO-nis). 48,332 sq. mi.; pop. 4,295,000, *ca.* 1962.

Tunis (TOO-nis); pop. 680,000.
Sousse (SOO-sah); pop. 48,172.
Bizerte (be-ZIR-tah); pop. 46,681.

Yemen (el-YA-man). 75,000 sq. mi.; pop. about
5,000,000.

Sana (SUN-ah); pop. 60,000.
Taizz (ta-AHZ); pop. 16,000.

Appendix B

THE ARABIC ALPHABET

SYMBOL*			NAME	SIMILAR ENGLISH SOUND
		ا	A-lif	a
بـ	ـبـ	ب	beh	b
تـ	ـتـ	ت	teh	t
ثـ	ـثـ	ث	theh	th (s in Egypt)
جـ	ـجـ	ج	jeem	j (g in Egypt)
حـ	ـحـ	ح	ħah	ħ
خـ	ـخـ	خ	khah	kh
		د	dal	d
		ذ	thal	z (d in Egypt)
		ر	reh	r
		ز	zayn	z
سـ	ـسـ	س	seen	s
شـ	ـشـ	ش	sheen	sh
صـ	ـصـ	ص	sahd	s
ضـ	ـضـ	ض	dahd	d
		ط	tah	t
		ظ	thah	z

* Where three forms are given, the first (left) is used at the beginning of a word, the second in the middle, the third at the end.

SYMBOL			NAME	SIMILAR ENGLISH SOUND
ء	‍ﺌ	ع	ayn	ay
ﻍ	ﻎ	غ	řayn	ř
ﻑ	ﻒ	ف	feh	f
ﻕ	ﻖ	ق	qahf	q (' in Egypt, in most cases)
ﻙ	ﻚ	ﻚ	kaf	k
ﻝ	ﻞ	ل	lam	l
ﻡ	ﻢ	م	meem	m
ﻥ	ﻦ	ن	noon	n
ﻩ	ﻪ	ه	heh	h
		و	wow	w (o)
ﻱ	ﻲ	ى	yeh	y (i, e)

PRESENT TENSE FORMS OF COMMONLY USED VERBS

MEANING	I	HE	WE	THEY
Answer	a-GA-wib	yi-GA-wib	ni-GA-wib	yi-GOW-boo
Ask	AS-al	YIS-al	NIS-al	yis-AL-loo
Bargain	ah-FAH-sill	yi-FAH-sill	ni-FAH-sill	yi-FAHS-loo
Breathe	at-NUF-fis	yit-NUF-fis	nit-NUF-fis	yit-nuf-FI-soo
Borrow	as-TE-lif	yis-TE-lif	nis-TE-lif	yis-TEL-foo
Buy	ash-TE-ree	yish-TE-ree	nish-TE-ree	yish-TE-roo
Call	a-NA-dee	yi-NA-dee	ni-NA-dee	yi-NA-doo
Close	A'-fill	YI'-fill	NI'-fill	yi'-FI-loo
Come	A-gee	YEE-gee	NEE-gee	YEE-goo
Count	AH-sib	YEH-sib	NEH-sib	yeh-SI-boo
Drink	ASH-rub	YISH-rub	NISH-rub	yish-RUB-boo
Drive	a-SOO'	yi-SOO'	ni-SOO'	yi-SOO-oo

MEANING	I	HE	WE	THEY
Eat	A-kŭll	YA-kŭll	NA-kŭll	YAK-loo
Find	a-LA-ee	yi-LA-ee	ni-LA-ee	yi-LA-oo
Forget	AN-sa	YIN-sa	NIN-sa	YIN-soo
Give	AD-dee	YID-dee	NID-dee	YID-doo
Go	ah-ROOĦ	yi-ROOĦ	ni-ROOĦ	yi-ROO-ĥoo
Have	AHN-dee	AHN-doh	ahn-DA-ha	ahn-DOH-hŭm
Hear	AS-mah	YIS-mah	NIS-mah	yis-MAH-oo
Know	AH-ruff	YI-ruff	NI-ruff	yi-RUF-foo
Lift	a-SHEEL	yi-SHEEL	ni-SHEEL	yi-SHEE-loo
Live	ah-EESH	yi-EESH	ni-EESH	yi-EE-shoo
Love	a-HEBB	yi-HEBB	ni-HEBB	yi-HEB-boo
Make	AH-mill	YI-mill	NI-mill	yi-MIL-loo
Meet	a-A-bill	yi-A-bill	ni-A-bill	yi-AB-loo
Open	AF-taĥ	YIF-taĥ	NIF-taĥ	yif-TA-ĥoo
Pass	ah-AHD-dee	yi-AHD-dee	ni-AHD-dee	yi-AHD-doo
Pay	AD-fah	YID-fah	NID-fah	yid-FAH-oo

MEANING	I	HE	WE	THEY
Quarrel	at-KHA-ni'	yit-KHA-ni'	nit-KHA-ni'	yit-KHAN-oo
Read	A'-rah	YI'-rah	NI'-rah	YI'-roo
Remember	af-TI-ker	yif-TI-ker	nif-TI-ker	yif-TIK-roo
Run	AG-ree	YIG-ree	NIG-ree	YIG-roo
See	a-SHOOF	yi-SHOOF	ni-SHOOF	yi-SHOO-foo
Sell	a-BEE-yah	yi-BEE-yah	ni-BEE-yah	yi-BEE-oo
Send	AB-aht	YIB-aht	NIB-aht	yib-AH-too
Sleep	a-NAM	yi-NAM	ni-NAM	yi-NA-moo
Smell	a-SHIM	yi-SHIM	ni-SHIM	yi-SHIM-moo
Smoke	ah-DAKH-ahn	yi-DAKH-ahn	ni-DAKH-ahn	yi-da-KHAH-noo
Speak	at-KAL-lim	yit-KAL-lim	nit-KAL-lim	yit-kal-LI-moo
Swim	a-OOM	yi-OOM	ni-OOM	yi-OO-moo
Take	AH-khŭd	YA-khŭd	NA-khŭd	YAKH-doo
Taste	a-DOO'	yi-DOO'	ni-DOO'	yi-DOO-oo
Think	ah-FAHK-ker	yi-FAHK-ker	ni-FAHK-ker	yi-fahk-KAH-roo
Travel	a-SA-fir	yi-SA-fir	ni-SA-fir	yi-SAF-roo

MEANING	I	HE	WE	THEY
Swear	AH-lif	YIH-lif	NIH-lif	yih-LI-foo
Wait	as-TAN-na	yis-TAN-na	nis-TAN-na	yis-TAN-noo
Wake up	AS-hah	YIS-hah	NIS-hah	YIS-hoo
Walk	AM-shee	YIM-shee	NIM-shee	YIM-shoo
Write	AK-tib	YIK-tib	NIK-tib	yik-TI-boo

INDEX

All the sentences, words and phrases in this book are numbered consecutively from 1 to 1462. The entries in this index refer to these numbers. In addition, each major section heading (capitalized) is indexed according to page number. Parts of speech are indicated (where there might be confusion) by the following italic abbreviations: *adj.* for adjective, *adv.* for adverb, *conj.* for conjunction, *n.* for noun, and *v.* for verb. Parentheses are used for explanations.

NOTE: Certain prepositions, possessive words and object pronouns are expressed in Arabic by prefixes and suffixes that fuse with their noun, sometimes modifying its form. Examples of such word elements are the prefixes *bee-* (with) and *lee-* (to) and the suffixes *-ee* (my) and *-k* (your). Wherever a noun appears in the numbered sentences combined with these prefixes and suffixes, the index entry shows the precise form that is used: e.g.: "aunt (my)," "twin beds (with)."

PUBLIC NOTICES

رجال	سيدات	ادفع	اجذب
MEN	LADIES	PUSH	PULL

دخول	خروج	طوارىء	خطر
ENTRANCE	EXIT	EMERGENCY	DANGER

خالى	مشغول	مفتوح	مغلق
VACANT	OCCUPIED	OPEN	CLOSED

بريد	تليفون	قسم شرطة
POST	TELEPHONE	POLICE STATION

وصول	قيام	شباك التذاكر
ARRIVAL	DEPARTURE	TICKET WINDOW

استعلامات	بنك	لوكانده (فندق)	مطعم
INFORMATION	BANK	HOTEL	RESTAURANT

عياده	دكتور (طبيب)	صيدلية (اجزخانة)
CLINIC	PHYSICIAN	PHARMACY

الثمن	للبيع	(شقة) للإيجار
PRICE	FOR SALE	(APARTMENT) FOR RENT

ممنوع التدخين	ممنوع الدخول	ممنوع المرور
NO SMOKING	NO ADMITTANCE	NO TRESPASSING

ممنوع البصق	ممنوع التصوير	ممنوع السير على الخضره
NO SPITTING	NO PHOTOGRAPHING	KEEP OFF GRASS